The Hallowed Howls of Congress

By
Roger H. Zion
Former U.S. Representative
Eighth District, Indiana

Guild Press of Indiana, Inc.
Indianapolis, Indiana

Guild Press of Indiana, Inc.
6000 Sunset Lane
Indianapolis, IN 46208

Printed in the United States of America

Library of Congress
Catalogue Card Number
94-081252

ISBN 1-878208-40-3

UNITED STATES SENATE
OFFICE OF THE REPUBLICAN LEADER
WASHINGTON, D. C.

BOB DOLE
KANSAS

My old friend, Roger Zion, has written
the perfect Washington book: funny, short,
and--most important of all, it doesn't have
an index--guaranteeing that people will read
every page and not just the ones containing
their name.

After much searching, I found my name in
a few stories.   I am confident that those
who take the time to search for those stories
will enjoy Roger's book as much as I did.

BOB DOLE

With the timing of a stand-up comedian and the memory of an elephant (Republican), my old friend and colleague, Roger Zion, has written a warm, witty, and, at times, wacky memoir filled with anecdotes, one-liners, and legendary tales about various Presidents, House members of both parties and both sexes, Senators, statesmen, golfers, and the folks back home in Indiana.

There is also serious material, such as the record of Roger's conversations with the North Vietnamese about the treatment of American POWs in 1970. Roger's gift for seeing the political world just a a bit off-center gives his book a wonderful, light-hearted quality. A true environmentalist of humor, he is not above recycling some old, old jokes, but they sound better than ever the way Roger tells them.

All in all, The Hallowed Howls of Congress *is funnier than anything I've read recently, including* The Congressional Record*!"*

Congressman Robert Michel

New Congressman Roger Zion (R-Ind.) is sworn into public service by Speaker of the House John McCormick, January, 1967.

Chapter One

I was born at an early age in Escanaba, Michigan, but I moved to Indiana as soon as I heard about it. In the last seventy years I have had a terrific time, but the most special period of my life was the four terms I spent in Congress—1966 to 1974.

Mark Twain said that there is no distinctly native American criminal class except Congress. You will enjoy the other side of the coin. I've been on a Navy ship, in many civic clubs, part of a large corporate organization, and a member of Congress. I found more hard-working, dedicated, honest, civic citizens in Congress than in any group with which I have been associated. The members also have a whole lot of fun. A bronze statue of Will Rogers, Oklahoma cowboy, philosopher, wit, and congressional critic, faces the door of the House of Representatives. Rogers once said, "Congress is a source of constant mirth and merriment."

It is that Congress I am writing about. I dedicate this book to my many friends and colleagues who lived these stories with me.

I Get Drafted

Many people have a deep-seated need to get into politics. I got dragged in.

One day early in 1964, Robert D. Orr called me. Bob was the Republican county chairman for Vanderburgh County. He later became a state senator, lieutenant governor, governor, and eventually, ambassador to Singapore.

He wanted me to run for Congress because I had a high profile in Evansville and no Republican had been elected in my district in 12 years. I told Bob, "No way." I liked my job as director of training and professional relations for Mead Johnson and Co., a leading manufacturer of nutrition and pharmaceutical products. Besides, I had no interest or ability in politics, and just plain didn't feel that it was my line. My wife, Marjorie, and I were enjoying our three children, each of whom was setting swimming records at our country club and doing well in school.

1

My old tennis partner later became the Honorable Robert D. Orr, governor of Indiana. That's me on the left.

Now Bob was a neighbor of my boss and company president, Daniel Mead Johnson, with whom I worked closely. The next day, Mead (as we called him) came into my office and informed me that he had started a finance campaign among his friends, had some great ideas about the campaign, and had arranged for my assistants to take over for me. He felt strongly that our Congressman was controlled by the unions, and wanted to see a businessman representing our district.

I was in politics.

Barry Goldwater was our presidential candidate. I accompanied him on a railroad tour from one end of the district to the other. I thought he was a great American. For the whole campaign, I talked only about Goldwater. We both lost—big. I led him by more than 20,000 votes and still lost. For the next two years I campaigned almost full time.

An Angel Appears

I started my campaign in an old building that was to be torn down after the election. It was an old two-story office building with a few desks but otherwise abandoned.

One day I was sitting at one of the desks wondering why in the world I was in this business when I heard someone coming up the stairs. It was a young woman in her mid-twenties. "I hear you need a press secretary," she said.

"I certainly do," I responded. "I also need a campaign manager, a few hundred workers, some promotional materials and lots of other things, but I'm afraid I won't have any money to pay for them."

"That's O.K.," she assured me. "Let's get this campaign off the ground; you can pay me when we get some money. First you have to get some exposure. I'll get started on that."

Her name was Angela Harris and she had been a teacher in Florida. Lucky for me, she had decided she'd rather be in public relations, and returned to her home in Evansville. Within a couple of days, Angela had borrowed a typewriter and a good-looking Chevrolet van. She designed an elephant with my name on it, had a friend cut

My press secretary, Angela Harris, and I (on right) exchange pleasantries with news commentator Chet Huntley. Angela invited Huntley to speak to the Washington Press Club.

it out of plywood and installed it on the roof of the van. Then she typed up a news release saying what a great Congressman I would be, and toured the district, stopping in every town that had a radio station or newspaper. She got acquainted with the media personnel and found out when they wanted news releases, what form they preferred, and who to contact when we had a story. She found out when all the local county fairs would be held and when there would be parades or other local events that would draw a crowd.

In the meantime, I had lined up a bunch of high schoolers who had an interest in politics. One of them, Randy Shephard, later became chief justice of the Indiana Supreme Court. Another, Don Elliott, became chief counsel of the Environmental Protection Agency. These youngsters became the "Young Citizens For Zion." Angela equipped them with straw hats with "Zion for Congress" on them and made sure they were conspicuous wherever there was a crowd.

The National GOP Looks Us Over

About halfway through the campaign, the national Republican Congressional Campaign Committee sent a field man down to Indiana to see how I was doing. His name was Ed Terrell. We frequently laugh about his reaction to the campaign.

"Let's see your campaign organization chart," he requested.

"Well, I really don't have it written down," I told him. "We have a very active group, though, that is getting the word out all over the district."

"Where are they now?" he asked.

"Up north handing out literature at a county fair," I told him. "I would be there but I'm giving a speech at a candidates' night."

"Who is your campaign manager?" he asked.

"A former school teacher named Angela," I told him.

"Who handles the publicity?" he asked.

"Well, Angela does," I replied. "She is also the head of "Young Citizens for Zion" and designs all the campaign literature."

That did it. Ed went back to Washington and reported what he saw. As a result, the Republican Congressional Campaign Committee decided there were a lot more viable campaigns than mine and sent their money to the candidates who had better organizations.

After I won that election in 1966, Bob Junk, my administrative assistant, hired Angela to be our press secretary. She became president of the Capitol Hill press secretaries' association and stayed with us until 1973, when President Richard M. Nixon asked her to head up the "Young Citizens for Nixon" campaign. After his re-election, Pat Nixon asked Angela to be her press secretary, but Angela declined and instead was appointed head of public relations for ACTION, the government agency that runs the Peace Corps, Job Corps and other similar organizations. She is now retired from public service, lives in Florida on a golf course, and has a swimming pool and three active sons.

In Indiana you get elected by shaking lots of hands. I did a lot of that. It also helps if you have a high-profile campaign. Thanks to all of the teenagers, we had that too.

One of my best campaigners was a young law student named Ted Yeiser, who felt so strongly that I should be elected, he offered to drop out of school for a semester to campaign full time. I talked him out of it.

The Feathers

Our campaign treasurer was a very creative guy from Jasper, Indiana, named Wayne Place. Wayne and Ted were always coming up with wild ideas. Like the time they decided to make Indian war bonnets out of turkey feathers. Jasper is in Dubois County, a great turkey-raising area. Wayne picked up a huge sack of feathers and brought them down to my campaign office. Then he had headbands printed with "Zion for Congress," which he planned to adorn with feathers. Ted was supposed to supply these to all the Republican booths at the county fairs, so that youngsters could come by and be fitted with "Indian headdresses."

It was a Saturday when Wayne bought the feathers, and he stuck them in a closet. By Monday morning, the office had a terrible stench.

The feathers had "ripened," and no one would go into the office for fear they would find a couple of dead bodies.

Ted and I thought we could solve the problem. We took the stinky feathers to a laundromat and shoved them in a washer with a lot of soap. When they finished the cycle we put them in a dryer and went down the street for a beer.

By the time we got back, the whole laundromat was filled with feathers. They had fluffed up, flown over the dryers, and scattered everywhere. It took us half a day to gather them up again.

During that time, four or five women came in to do their washing. We didn't explain a thing—just scooped up the feathers and giggled.

Dirksen Helps?

One of the most popular politicians in 1966 was the golden-voiced senator from Illinois, the late Everett Dirksen.

My people thought it would be a great boost to my campaign if Senator Dirksen would record radio and television promotional spots for me. They called him, he agreed, and, just four days before the election, we received the tape and film.

Elated, we rushed to the T.V. station to see his endorsement and schedule the commercial time. As we watched the venerable Everett looking directly into the camera and extolling my virtues, we were most impressed — until he wound up his presentation by saying, "You people in Southern Indiana would be fortunate if you elected Robert Zion to Congress."

Unfortunately, with Roger Zion's name on the ballot, Dirksen's endorsement of Robert Zion wouldn't help much.

Not to be completely undone, Marvin Lockyear, who had scheduled the commercial, took out a fingernail clipper, snipped the edge of the sound track at just the right spot, and showed it to us again. This time, as Dirksen concluded his pitch, his lips moved at the name "Robert" but his voice was silent. The people of Southern Indiana were treated to an enthusiastic request to elect _____ Zion.

"Do we really have to do this, Dad?" My children, Randy 10; Scott, 13; and Gayle, 15, prove they'll go to almost any lengths to help dear old Dad in 1964, although not always thrilled about it.

One way to attract attention is to get a van, put a big plywood elephant on top and drive around—and that's just what we did during my successful 1966 campaign, thanks to my campaign manager, Angela Harris.

The Election

On election day, I drove around to as many precincts as I could. Young supporters were wearing my hats and handing out literature at each precinct, and I wanted to thank them.

The senior political writer at the Evansville Press was Bob Flynn. Bob found a precinct that had correctly predicted the election for years — a "bellwether." He called on the voters a couple of days before the election and found that the vote was to be very close.

The last precinct I visited before the polls closed was the Flynn bellwether. As votes were tabulated, it appeared that I had won by a slim margin. My people were excited.

We went down to the campaign headquarters and waited for the results to come in from the neighboring counties. By 3:00 a.m., it was evident that I had squeezed by. I earned the title, "Ol' Landslide Zion."

Two years and thousands of hours of work from dedicated supporters had resulted in the upset victory of the year.

I Meet the Junk Man

My upset victory was a big surprise to a lot of people—including me! Since I had no previous interest and certainly no experience in the business, I was not too sure what was expected of me.

Up in the northern part of the state, Congressman Ralph Harvey had been defeated in a primary race with Richard Roudebush. These two Republicans had been put in the same congressional district by the state legislature and had to face each other in the primary election.

I didn't know Harvey but called him to see if he had any lame duck staff people that I could hire. "Who's left?" I asked.

"Bob Junk," he replied.

"What's he do?" I asked.

"Well, Bob does most everything. He used to publish a small weekly paper in Indiana. He joined me as a press aide. Right now he is running the whole office."

"Put him on," I asked. Bob got on the phone. "How do you spell your name?" I asked.

"J-U-N-K," Bob responded. "A common household name. You find it everywhere."

I asked him if he had found a job. He said he hadn't had time to look since he was winding up the casework, finishing up the paperwork and packing some papers that were going to Indiana University.

"How would you like to be my A.A.?" I asked, referring to the job of administrative assistant. "OK," he replied.

That was that. I figured if a guy was that loyal to Ralph Harvey, he would be the same to me. Besides, he had good experience in most phases of the job. I explained to Bob that I was finishing some consulting work and wouldn't be able to come to Washington until time for the swearing-in ceremony in January. I told him that he was to select the office, hire the staff and be ready for me when the 90th Congress assembled. He agreed.

Actually I dropped in for a couple of hours a week before I was expected. A national advertising group selected an "upset victor of the year" each election cycle and invited him to their annual convention in Washington to explain how he overcame the big odds. I was their "upset victor" for 1966.

I arranged for flights that arrived in the morning and left in the afternoon, with just enough time to appear at the meeting and meet with Bob briefly. I called him and asked him to drop by the hotel later and fill me in on how he was doing.

At the convention, I showed some of my campaign materials and explained how we recruited hundreds of teenagers, who created such a scene at public events that people favorably identified me with youth and action, in contrast to my older opponent.

As I was leaving the hall, a rather unassuming fellow tapped me on the shoulder. "I'm Junk," he said. So we met for the first time. He drove me to the airport and gave me an update on his progress. Since I didn't know anything about a congressional office, I couldn't comment on what he was doing.

When I arrived the morning of the swearing-in ceremony, I asked a Capitol policeman to direct me to the Longworth Office

Building. I saw my name on the directory and took the elevator to the second floor.

When I got to my office, it was fully staffed. My new group had managed to purloin the best office furniture on the floor, and there was a stack of mail on my desk, all answered and ready for my signature.

My snap judgment about an A.A. paid off. For the next eight years, I had one of the smoothest, most productive offices on Capitol Hill.

Fishbait Helps

Most members bring their families to Washington for their introduction to the Capitol, and I was no exception. I brought my wife and three children, and my parents flew down from Milwaukee for the momentous occasion. The only hitch was that each member only received four passes to the House Gallery to watch the proceedings, and I needed six. Junk suggested that maybe "Fishbait" Miller, the Doorkeeper, might have an extra ticket or two, so I called on him and explained that my boys were without access to this important event. "How old are they?" Fishbait asked. (Incidentally, when Miller first got a job on Capitol Hill, House Speaker Sam Rayburn said he was no bigger than fishbait, and the name stuck).

Well, I told him that Randy was thirteen and Scott was fifteen years old. "What a coincidence," Miller said. "I need two honorary pages today."

He arranged for them to come in with me, but they had to stand near my seat at the end of a row. Randy was a big fan of Bob Mathias, the great decathlon champion, and was excited to see him being sworn in as a freshman Congressman just three rows in front of us.

Scott had a great experience, too. Before the swearing-in ceremony, there was a period to ask any member to step aside if there was any question of his eligibility. Some member suggested that Fletcher Thompson of Georgia had some election irregularities and should step aside. The House voted to seat him because the Georgia secretary of state had affirmed his eligibility.

Then came the question of Adam Clayton Powell, the embattled member from New York. Powell had been an absentee member of Congress, and had been accused of stealing a staffer's house, having ghost employees, receiving payroll kickbacks, and other offenses.

We all heard one of the greatest speeches of all time.

Albert Watson of South Carolina had once been a warm-up speaker for an evangelist. He was fabulous!! His famous anti-Powell speech was a show-stopper. He wound up with, "When we had all these problems in Washington, when we needed every member to attend to his duties and work for his country, where was Adam? I'll tell you where he was. He was in Bimini with a babe in one arm and a bottle in the other."

While Watson was making his great speech, Powell was roaming the floor. He stopped by Scott, put his arm on his shoulder and asked "How do you think this is going?"

Scott didn't hesitate a second. "I think you've had it, sir," he told him.

Scott was right. In a precedent-setting procedure, the House declared that it had the final right to pass on the eligibility of its members. Adam Clayton Powell's political career was over.

I Meet Jerry Ford

On my first day in office, it was suggested that I call on the House Minority Leader, Gerald R. Ford. Representative John Myers, a fellow freshman from Indiana, went with me. We went to Ford's office in the Capitol. He was delighted to meet his new members and asked what committee assignments we wanted. "I'd like Foreign Affairs," I told him.

"Sorry, Indiana has the ranking member, Ross Adair," Ford said. Adair was a Fourth District Republican.

"How about Armed Services?" I asked.

"Nope, you have Bill Bray (a Sixth District Republican)."

Commerce? "Well, we have an opening on Commerce, but Don Brotzman of Colorado is a second-term member and he requested Commerce."

Jerry Ford is one of the nicest and most sincere men I've ever known.

"So what are you giving me?" I asked.

"One of you gets Agriculture and one, Public Works," we were told.

John and I looked at each other. "I don't know a thing about farming," I told him. "Could you take Ag?" The truth is that I didn't know anything about Public Works either. Myers took Agriculture and I wound up on the Public Works Committee.

It proved to be a good assignment for me. The committee considers funding proposals for bridges, highways and public buildings, as well as flood control projects. My district was in a corner of Indiana bounded by the Ohio and Wabash Rivers. As I later told the Army Corps of Engineers, "If it weren't for you guys, my constituents would have webbed feet."

The Honorable Roger Zion

By the time new Congressmen arrive in Washington, the Capitol Police have seen and memorized their pictures. They stop traffic for them, call them by name, salute, and generally make them feel very important. On the Senate side, which is 240 feet north of the House and five light-years away in prestige, they don't need special police treatment to feel important. Those elected officials think of themselves as the House of Lords.

There's a haberdashery shop on the Senate side of Capitol Hill where hat sizes average about 8 1/2.

Members of Congress are treated as kings by their staffs. Lobbyists wine and dine them and make campaign contributions. D.C. police let them park anywhere they want. They get to go to parties at the White House. No wonder some of them get the big head. I'm an exception. I have kept my inherent modesty. My four terms in Congress, however, did give me an opportunity to gather material for my book, Presidents Who Have Known Me.

In the olden days, Eastern Airlines had a V.I.P. suite where congressmen, Supreme Court justices, movie stars, and other celebrities could have a drink and wait in comfort for their plane's departure.

I was sitting there with a couple of Congressmen from Kentucky when one of them asked me about my family.

I told him, in all modesty, about the superior intellectual and athletic capacity that they enjoyed. In fact I dwelled on the subject for quite a while.

When I finished, he started bragging about his kids. Then the other member wanted to be sure he wasn't outdone, and bored us with examples of his kid's accomplishments.

Some guy in the corner was obviously and visibly irritated by the whole discussion. I thought he wanted to join the brag-fest so I asked him if he had any children. "Yes I do," he responded. " Never married, but I have three children, all Congressmen."

Once, we were sitting in a plane waiting for departure when the captain came on the intercom and announced, "We will have a short delay while we are waiting for clearance." My companion, Representative Gene Snyder of Kentucky, was expected to make a commencement address and was impatient to get away. He strutted up to the flight deck and announced, "I'm Congressman Snyder. I'm ranking member on the Transportation Committee—patch me through to the Control Tower. By God, I'll get us clearance."

"No, no — not clearance," the captain explained, "I'm waiting for Clarence, the co-pilot."

The Interns

Many members have groups of students who work part-time in the Washington office during semester breaks. I usually had four or five at a time for a period of one month. Then another group came in.

It was a good experience for the students. They worked a half day in the office, answering mail, running errands, studying legislation and taking constituents around the Capitol. In the afternoon they toured Washington or attended seminars put on by Members of Congress or committee staff people. The intern was paid enough to cover his/her living expenses while in town. The money came from a special fund set up by President Lyndon B. Johnson during his ad-

These students, who served as legislative interns, will never forget their month in Washington.

ministration.

I had told my administrative assistant, Bob Junk, that he was supposed to handle all problems. When he was hired, I explained my management philosophy. "You are completely responsible for running the office. You do the hiring, the salary administration, the training and all other administrative functions."

When I delegated responsibility and authority for running the office, I felt free to do the traveling, the speaking, the voting, and all of the many activities that make up the usual fifty-to sixty-hour week.

One morning around 2:00 a.m., I received a phone call. It was Junk. "I know I'm not supposed to bother you with trivia," he began, "but two of our interns are in jail."

"Now Bob," I said, "That's your problem. I don't want to hear about it." Then I paused, thought about it for a minute and mumbled, "Who's in jail?"

"Well it's our two new lovelies," he replied. (That's what Bob called attractive young ladies when he couldn't remember their names.)

"Oops! What can I do?" I asked.

"Call this number," Bob replied. "Tell the officer in charge that you will take personal responsibility for these two women and I can take them home."

I did as I was told and the case was closed...almost. Though I really didn't want to know the circumstances, Bob's need to tell me, and my curiosity finally got the best of both of us and he confided in me (off the record) that the two lovelies had gone to the Hawk and Dove, a staff hang-out near Capitol Hill, for a late-evening beer.

Two attractive young men, who passed themselves off as Senate staff assistants, agreed to drive them home. Unfortunately, they weren't Senate staffers and they were driving a stolen car. They were intercepted by two (not one) squad cars and taken to the station house.

I presumed that the subject would never be brought up in the office, but I was wrong. The first thing next morning, I heard the interns' room buzzing. Obviously the whole story was being told with great gestures and giggles. The punch line was, "And all these policemen took us out of the car and frisked us—oooh wow!"

From that day on, every time something exciting happened in our office, the person explaining the event ended with, "oooh wow."

President George Bush visits the annual House gym party.

Me and George

One of my fellow freshman Congressmen was George Bush. It's amazing how parallel my career has been to his. We both graduated from college and joined the Navy as aviation cadets. We both completed flight training at about the same time. Of course we all know he became a hero as a dive bomber pilot. I would have been a hero, too, except that I was grounded for recklessness on one of our training flights and was transferred to the supply corps.

After the war, George started a successful oil business in Texas and I was a baby food salesman in Ohio. He made a lot of money and I made a lot of friends.

We were both elected to Congress in 1966, which was a great year for Republicans. Voters were so upset with Lyndon Johnson that most any Republican could be elected. George and I spent our rare leisure time in the House gym playing paddleball. He was a real "Hot Dog" — hit the ball behind his back, under his leg, etc. He was one of the best players. Bob Mathias, the two-time Olympic decathlon champion, played with us. Members had an informal rating system. The good players teamed up with the less accomplished. I got to have George as a partner often.

Yes, George and I have a lot in common. Our careers are very similar. He became President. I had to give up politics after four terms because of ill health. My constituents got sick of me.

Bill Cowger Played it Loose

Bill Cowger had been Mayor of Louisville, Kentucky, when he was elected to Congress in 1966. On Monday mornings, I caught an Eastern Airlines plane and headed for Washington, and Louisville was the only stop between the two stations. After Cowger and Congressman Gene Snyder got on at Louisville, we'd start a card game. We invented a three-handed gin rummy game and played on the way to and from Washington about every week. Bill also played paddleball in the gym, so I got to know him pretty well.

In 1966 we had a large freshman class of Congressmen. Two or three of the members campaigned very hard to be elected president of this freshman class. Some of us resented all this attention and felt we had more important things to do than to buttonhole each other and ask for support in the upcoming class election. Just prior to the election, some of us held a mini-caucus and decided to vote for the least interested member of the class. That was Bill. He hadn't campaigned at all and was a real "good ol' boy." So we elected him president of the class. He did a great job, too.

His wife, Sylvia, sort of shifted back and forth from their homes in Louisville and Washington, and was concerned about Bill's high living and what it would do to his health. He had a group of guys he called his "rat pack": they played golf, drank a bit of what Kentucky is famous for, and played gin rummy into the night.

Bill confided in Snyder and me that he had a heart problem, though his constituents thought he occasionally went to the hospital for the flu. For a man in his condition he lived a very vigorous life.

Once Bill was especially late coming home, and Sylvia met him at the door. "Where on Earth have you been?" she demanded.

"Well, Sylvia," Bill explained, "As I was leaving my office this evening I noticed this beautiful girl in the office next door. She was a real knockout. I introduced myself and took her out for a drink. We got hungry and went out to eat. After dinner, she invited me over for coffee. One thing led to another and before I noticed it was two o'clock in the morning."

"Don't you lie to me like that, Bill Cowger," Sylvia threatened. "You've been out playing gin rummy again."

Bill called it as he saw it. In 1969 he decided to run against Senator Thurston Morton, an entrenched member of his own party. Bill was a pretty aggressive campaigner and he offended a lot of people. He didn't endear himself to his Republican friends, either, when he made derogatory remarks about his state chairman. Just to be sure he passed the insults out to everyone, he called his largest newspaper a "scandal sheet" and said the worst thing that could happen would be to have an endorsement from that "left-wing rag."

Needless to say, he didn't win the nomination. He had turned so many people off that he also lost the next election for Congress. He died shortly after that. I remember saying about him in his eulogy on the House floor: "Bill was a man who lived while he lived and then died and was done with it." I think he would have liked that.

That's My Dad

Lyndon Johnson had a reception at the White House for new members of Congress. It was a nice affair and followed the usual protocol. Military honor guard members in white gloves greeted us at the reception room. A military band played show tunes. We were ushered up to the East Room, where waiters served drinks while we mingled, waiting for the President and Mrs. Johnson to "go into their act."

The usual procedure is for the first family to stand in a reception line with members of the Cabinet. As the members and their spouses file past (members first), the House doorkeeper introduces them. After all the guests have gone through the line, they flow into the Lincoln Dining Room. There is usually an hors d'oeuvres table, and additional drinks and snacks are passed around.

I was standing in a corner chatting with some other freshman members when an attractive, dark-haired girl came up to us. She was wearing a pants outfit with large black-and-white squares. She struck up a conversation and asked me what committees I was on.

"Public Works," I told her.

"That's roads and bridges and things like that, isn't it?" she asked.

"Yes" I expounded. "I wish we had more money to rebuild dangerous bridges," I told her.

"Why don't you ask Daddy?" she suggested.

"Who's Daddy?" I asked.

"Over there," she told me, pointing to the President, who was in an animated conversation with John Myers, freshman from Indiana.

Gulp! I was talking to Lynda Bird Johnson.

Johnson Waits

A later visit to the Johnson White House was much less pleasant. It was during the Vietnam War. Things weren't going well and the President wanted Congress to support his actions in that theater. If it hadn't been for Lady Bird, the reception might have gone better.

Lady Bird was a great environmentalist. First ladies usually have a project or two by which they are known. In her case, she supervised the planting of trees, flowers and bushes all around Washington. Much of the beauty of the capital city is a result of her enthusiastic beautification.

In order to extend her influence beyond the capital, she talked some members of the Public Works committee into adding several million dollars to a highway bill for a section to be known as the Lady Bird Highway Beautification Section.

We had experienced some difficulty with similar programs in the past. Cement flower bed rims that blocked access to stores and taverns were mysteriously broken. Shrubs in front of billboards died unnatural deaths. Flowers along roadsides were dug up and stolen. Evergreens by the hundreds were dug up or chopped down at Christmas time.

I wasn't against beautification, but I was terribly concerned about dozens of bridges around the country that were in a dangerous condition.

When the highway bill came to the floor, I put in an amendment to transfer the Lady Bird money to a "killer bridges" account. I guess I was pretty convincing, because the debate lasted late into the evening. Some of my old friends on the committee still call me "killer" because of my vigorous advocacy of the "killer bridges" amendment.

Finally the amendment was defeated after a prolonged vote during which many of Johnson's friends were "encouraged" to change their vote to support the beautification section.

Unfortunately, this late session was the same night that we were expected at the White House. By the time we arrived, Johnson was understandably upset. He had a bad cold, his critics were working him over on the Vietnam war, his reception was two hours late, and his wife's pet program was almost defeated.

Fellow Hoosier Charlie Halleck, House Minority Leader, would have made a great Speaker of the House if Republicans could have been in the majority.

He wasn't nearly as hospitable on this visit as he had been on previous ones.

Charlie's "Clinic"

There is a women's restroom in the Capitol that has suffered a serious demotion. Women who visit it don't know it, but this lowly toilet was once Charlie's "Clinic."

When I was elected, the ranking Republican in the House was a fellow Hoosier named Charlie Halleck. As a "perk" for his position he was given a special "hideaway" room in the Capitol. He could use it for any purpose that suited him. In this case, Charlie had it equipped with a refrigerator stocked with gin, five folding chairs, and a small table.

Charlie was a hunter and a fisherman. He would frequently bring the proceeds of his hunt to Washington to share with the Indiana delegation. He would take the fish, elk, ducks, or whatever to the Capitol dining room and tell the cooks how he wanted them prepared. Then his secretary would call our offices and invite us to lunch in the "clinic." It was a command performance and no excuse was big enough to avoid attendance.

There were three senior members of our delegation, and John Myers and me, the two freshmen. The seniors felt compelled to instruct John and me in the ways of Congress, and we, of course, were pleased to learn our new profession.

A.B.C.s of Politics

Charlie had some good advice. He told John and me to "always go home from the dance with the girl who brung you." He explained that this means we should remember who worked on our campaign, who contributed money, who hosted fundraising receptions, etc. He also reminded us that there were groups that worked against us and that we shouldn't be expected to support their legislative requests.

Incidentally, Bill Bray had two pieces of advice. One was to always vote "no" if there was any doubt about which way to go. He said that when someone asked him why he supported some specific legislation, it took a long time to explain. He said it was easier to answer a "no" vote. "Anyone who would vote for that bucket of guts is nuts." he would say. That usually satisfied the inquirer. His second rule was that "you never get beat by the speech you didn't make." He explained that in every campaign, someone will select a part of a news release, or a passage in the Congressional Record, and use it against you. The only way to keep from being misquoted is to not say anything in the first place. Both John and I wished dozens of times that we had followed his advice.

The Baited Field

Once Charlie was charged with shooting ducks over a baited field. Even though the practice is illegal, some hunters will throw out corn or other bird food to attract birds, and then shoot them. The story made headlines because Charlie was pretty famous. He and Senator Everett Dirksen had a weekly "Ev and Charlie" radio show, and a lot of people listened to it.

Charlie, of course, was a bit upset about his arrest and hoped that it would be forgotten. John Myers and I saw to it that it wouldn't be. We got a stuffed duck, handcuffed it to a plank and glued some corn under its beak. It was waiting for him when he returned to his "clinic".

I understand that our duck, together with many cartoons that were published about Charlie and Ev and other mementos of the clinic, are preserved in a museum at Indiana University.

Charlie and Ike

Though the rest of us usually faked drinking Charlie's martinis, he really sipped a few of them during our meetings. We knew it was time to leave (if we could do so graciously) when he started reminiscing about his relationship with Dwight Eisenhower.

25

As Charlie remembered it, Ike wanted to challenge Bob (Mr. Republican) Taft for the Presidential nomination in the Chicago convention of 1952. Charlie was a very well known and respected member of the Republican Party. Ike told Charlie that he would be his running mate if Charlie would make the nomination speech at the Republican convention.

Charlie made the speech, Ike was nominated, and Ike took Richard Nixon as his running mate. Charlie never got over it.

The Young Turks

In 1968 a group of "young turks" thought that Charlie was too conservative to be the head of the House Republicans and campaigned against him. These were well-respected members such as Mel Laird of Wisconsin, Al Quie of Minnesota and Charlie Goodell of New York

Their candidate was Jerry Ford, a very popular member from Michigan. Of course, Ford was elected. Charlie retired the next year, ending a very productive political career.

Quie later was elected governor of Minnesota, Goodell was appointed to succeed John Kennedy Jr. as senator from New York, and Jerry Ford eventually became President. Mel Laird became his secretary of defense.

Bayh And Bought

I was never very fond of Indiana's two Democratic senators, R. Vance Hartke and Birch Bayh, but I liked them even less when we made appearances together. Whenever an Indiana group came to Washington, they would invite members of the delegation to speak. Hartke or Bayh would speak first. I could give their pitch for them, I heard it so often. They always promised the constituents everything — free dentures, free hearing aids, free rent, free medical care, shorter hours, more pay, etc. After they received thunderous applause, I was called on. By then, everything had been promised. All I could do was talk about the national debt, inflation (the cruelest tax of all), and the need to maximize the productive use of our manpower, money, markets, and materials. Of course, the few people who stayed around for my talk did so because they had fallen asleep.

Mark Russell, a great comedic entertainer, called it like it was. Russell started out playing piano and spoofing Washington at a little bar on Capitol Hill, and graduated to the Shoreham Hotel. One night I took some constituents to see him perform. He had checked the guest list and knew a Congressman from Indiana was in the house. As part of his act, he mentioned, "Well, we have a Congressman from Indiana. That's the state famous for its two senators, Buy and Bought."

I once made a small ripple in a national magazine. Many folks thought my comments were rather droll and sent copies of the article to me. It stated: Vance Hartke's popular appeal to the average voter was summed up a few years ago by then-Representative Roger Zion of Evansville. In 1972, Hartke took a brief shot at the presidency, perhaps to satisfy his larger-than-normal ego. He campaigned vigorously in New Hampshire, trudged through snow, trying to "reach every voter." When the results of the nation's first primary were in, Hartke had garnered a grand total of three percent of the votes. Congressman Zion was interviewed on an Indiana television station shortly after and was asked to comment on Hartke's dismal showing.

"I must compliment Vance on his campaigning," Zion said. "He reached 97 percent of the people!"

Super Mooch

The first time I can remember meeting Vance Hartke, he was the mayor of Evansville. A group of us had founded a dance club called "Cotillion." We met once a month, hired a band and enjoyed an evening of dancing.

One evening, several of us were standing around during an intermission. Vance walked up and introduced himself. "Sure I know you," the president of the club replied. "You're the only guy who hasn't paid his dues."

I learned through the years that Hartke didn't mind being put down. He seemed to enjoy it. It was said of him that he didn't mind what people thought of him or what appeared in the press. "Just spell the name right," he reportedly said, "and mention me often."

When Hartke first ran for the U.S. Senate in 1958 he probably shook more hands in Indiana than any candidate in history. He attended football, basketball and soccer games. He met people at lunches, shopping centers and anywhere people gathered. I once saw him working a crowd at a huge stadium. He started at the top row and shook hands with everyone in the place. He did anything he could to attract attention.

Indy Boos

While Vance was a member of the U.S. Senate, he was the VIP guest at the Indianapolis 500-Mile Race. He rode in the pace car. I remember an announcer who was reporting the race saying, "You can tell where the pace car is as it travels the route, by the boos in the stands."

Super Put-Down

Every Christmas a group of Indianapolis businessmen threw a party in Washington for Hoosier friends. It was a very nice affair and cost them quite a bundle, so they issued invitations selectively. Hartke always used this as a vehicle to repay social obligations, and brought a crowd of people with him.

The hosts resented this and left him off the guest list one year. It didn't do a bit of good. Hartke called around, found out when the party was to be held, and showed up with his usual groupies.

At one of these parties, I was talking to some of Congressman Bud Hillis' staff people when Hartke walked up. Bud had a young receptionist who caught Hartke's eye. "What is your name, young lady?" he asked.

"Betsy," she replied.

"And where are you from?" he persisted.

"Kokomo," she answered.

"I hear that girls from Kokomo are the prettiest, sexiest and friendliest in the country," Hartke continued.

"Horse shit, Vance," she exploded.

I almost dropped my drink. The guy who always set himself up for ridicule got the perfect put-down.

Who Gets the Tab?

One of Washington's most expensive restaurants is the Prime Rib. It is one of the "Power Spots" where people go to see and be seen. I was there as the guest of a friend from Evansville who wanted to visit the capital's better restaurants.

Just as we were about to order, Hartke walked in with a couple of friends. "Hi, Roger," he greeted me. "Mind if we join you?"

I was about to protest, but my friend was pleased to have the distinguished senator at our table, so he invited them to sit down. The waiter had to bring an extra chair to accommodate the five of us. We all ordered.

After a pleasant dinner, during which Hartke extolled his many virtues and accomplishments, he and his two guests thanked us for the dinner and left us with the check.

Inaugural Push-In

When Richard Nixon was sworn in as President for a second term in 1973, there were a lot of inaugural balls in Washington. Republican leaders from around the country put on black ties and congregated at various hotels to celebrate at a Republican reception. Hartke (a Democrat) greeted all the guests as they came through the door at one hotel. You would have thought he was giving the party.

Indiana was assigned a hotel for its ball and we got ready to "put on the dog." As is the usual procedure, the state Republican dignitaries stood in a reception line and greeted the party faithful. It was a long line: Governor and Mrs. Otis R. Bowen, Lt. Governor and Mrs.

Robert Orr, the seven Republican congressmen with wives and/or family members. Our son, Scott, who was in his early twenties, showed just how ridiculous these formalities could be. He stood in the reception line and, as each guest came by, extended his hand and introduced himself, using a different name each time. "I'm Red Grange," he would say, or "Pavo Nermi," or "Jimmy Stewart," or "Max Baer." No one even did a double-take. They just said "Hi, Pavo," or whatever, and proceeded down the line.

About halfway through the reception, Martha Hartke rushed in and shoved her way between Beth Bowen and Josie Orr. "I'm sorry Vance isn't here," she apologized. "He had another commitment."

Josie Orr drew herself up to her considerable height and asked, "Just who the hell are you?" It didn't faze Martha a bit. She, like Vance, was completely immune to insults. They wanted to be noticed, regardless of what they had to do.

Sun Hazards

One day Hartke and I were participating in a groundbreaking ceremony for a senior citizens' home. The event was held in a country field. A flatbed trailer had been moved to the site and chairs were set up for all the officials. It was a hot summer day.

Senator Hartke was selected to speak first. Had he not been there, I could have made his speech for him. "Senior citizens are the most important folks in the country. They should have free rent, free dentures, free food, etc., etc."

It seemed that he ran on much more that usual and he was never accused of being short-winded. Everyone was hot, especially those of us on the platform. I almost always wear a hat to protect my bald head from getting skin cancer. This day I had forgotten to bring one.

Finally Hartke looked at me and admitted, "I've talked longer than usual to see how red Zion's head would get."

The last time I saw Hartke was after both of us had been "retired" from Congress. Both of us had become consultants, and we met on the street in Washington. He was his usual, very friendly self.

"Hi ol' friend," he greeted me. "What are you up to?" Hartke and Birch Bayh were always very cordial when they met me. Then they would cut me up behind my back. Bayh and Sen. Edward Kennedy, plus several other left-wing senators, once signed a fundraising letter to "get rid of the ten most dangerous congressmen," and I was on the list. I asked Bayh at an Indiana delegation meeting why he considered me dangerous, and he completely denied knowing that such a letter had gone out.

I was always suspicious of both of them, so I didn't offer much information when Hartke wondered what I was up to.

"We should do business together," Hartke said. "Here's my phone number. Notice it ends in 5050. That's how we'll split the fee, 50/50. Give me a call and we'll get together."

I never called him.

Chapter Two

It was said that Jim Farley, postmaster general under Franklin Roosevelt, was one of our greatest politicians. He was great because he met hundreds of people and had a tremendous ability to remember names.

Speaker Thomas P. O'Neill, Jr. was a lot like Farley in that respect. About a year after our congressional golf tournament I saw "Tip" in action. We were in the house gym. O'Neill frequently came down for a steam bath. He was talking to a former member who hadn't been around for at least ten years. Tip knew his name, where he was from, his wife's name, and the details of his life.

After talking to him, Tip came up to me and asked, "How did you and Laird come out in your game with Cederberg and Harsha last summer?"

I hardly remembered with whom I played, much less who had won, but I had a special appreciation of Tip's memory and interest.

Wherever the Speaker went, he had a big entourage of reporters, staff, or members with him. He was never too busy to talk to visitors, though. I know that I introduced him to at least a dozen of my friends or constituents. If Tip saw that you wanted him to meet someone, he would leave his pack of people, extend his hand and say, "Hi! I'm Tip O'Neill." That then gave me a chance to point out that "you have just met the second most powerful man in the world."

It didn't hurt either one of us.

The Nut File

I didn't know it, but my staff kept a file called "the nut file." It was made up of all kinds of loony letters. Some of them were threatening. Copies of those letters were sent to the F.B.I.

It was fortunate that they were, because during the Vietnam war, I made some hawkish speeches. Later I learned that F.B.I. agents were at these gatherings and were monitoring anyone who had written threatening letters to me.

One friendly letter-writer was Dory Chuttinger, from a little town in Southern Indiana. She wrote long, newsy letters, telling me all that went on in her neighborhood. My chief caseworker, Rosie, always wrote back, commenting on her letter and telling her what I was doing. I signed the letters and we became pen pals.

One of her letters asked me to contact the Veterans Administration. She told in great detail how lonely she was, and how she hoped I could get the V.A. to send her a veteran for company.

Our paths finally crossed when I was scheduled to ride in a parade in DuBois county, and a notice was put in the local paper. Dory wrote to me saying she would be curbside, wearing a print dress and a flowered hat.

As the parade rounded the corner, I saw a woman in a print dress and a hat with big flowers on it. I jumped out of the convertible and embraced her. Dory and I had finally met.

How Not to Be Conned

The first time I met Walter Dilbeck was in 1964 when I made my first run for Congress. Walter, the quintessential promoter, summoned me to his office, which was the bridal suite of the McCurdy hotel. It even had a bed on a raised platform. Walter had a pencil-line mustache and a glib tongue. He was the kind of guy who could sell a milking machine to a farmer and take his only cow as a down payment. He wished me well in my campaign and gave me a hundred-dollar bill. This sort of surprised me since he had run for mayor of Evansville as a Democrat, but I figured he worked both sides of the street in case he wanted a favor sometime later.

How right I was.

The first time I heard from him was a bit exciting. My secretary came in and announced that I was to stand by for a conference call with Bing Crosby and Bob Hope. I asked who originated the call and she told me it was Walter Dilbeck.

Something told me that I should not be available when the call came in. But every time the phone rang, everyone else in the office picked up their extension so they could hear Bing and Bob.

Apparently Walter had called the two superstars and asked them to stand by for a call from Congressman Zion. When the operator asked for me and was told I wasn't available, the whole thing fell through.

I seems that Walter had organized a global baseball team. He lined up a team of recently retired big-name players and hired them to play exhibition games in foreign countries. He wanted Crosby and Hope to finance the deal, but he knew they wouldn't return his calls. So, he used me, figuring they'd be more likely to call a U.S. Congressman. When that fell through, he obtained some minimum financing somewhere and took off with his team, hoping that gate receipts would pay the bills.

The next time I heard from him, a call came person-to-person for me from Puerto Rico.

I picked up the phone and there was Walter.

"Here's what I want you to do, Roger," he explained. "Call Dick and tell him to send $40,000 to the hotel in San Juan."

"Who's Dick?" I asked.

"Why Nixon, of course," he responded. "We are in an embarrassing situation down here that reflects badly on the United States. If we don't pay our hotel bill, we'll all go to jail."

I told Walter that I didn't know "Dick" that well and that he was on his own. I figured that was the last I would hear from him.

I was wrong.

One afternoon he called for me and was told I wasn't available. "Let me talk to someone else then," he demanded.

Belden Bell, my very capable legislative assistant, took up the phone. "What can we do for you, Walter?" he asked.

"Tell Roger I want him to come to my Reagan for President office on East Capitol Street this evening."

"What do you want him to do?" Beldon asked.

"Just stand around," he was told.

I declined.

The next day I sat next to Jimmy Utt, a representative from California. "How well do you know Governor Ronald Reagan?" I asked him.

"Real well," he responded.

The most sought-after speaker in the United States—California Governor Ronald Reagan—came to campaign for me. Of course, he went on to even bigger and better things.

I suggested that he call the governor, tell him about Dilbeck's office, and suggest that the Hoosier's efforts might not result in any money contributed to the Reagan presidential campaign. He gave Reagan a call. The next day Governor Reagan put out a press release for the Washington media, disclaiming any connection with the Dilbeck office.

That ended that.

Walter never gave up. One day he walked into the office with a distinguished-looking man, who was introduced as a Hollywood director who was to direct the "Walter Dilbeck Story." Walter wanted us to help raise money for the project. It was a short visit.

In his declining days, Walter suffered from ill health and devoted his time and considerable enthusiasm working for his church. He died in 1990. I often wonder what sort of a deal he made with St. Peter.

"Vinegar Bend"

One of the greatest storytellers I've ever heard is Wilmer Mizell. He grew up near Vinegar Bend, South Carolina, thus the nickname. He was a tall, skinny kid who could throw a baseball like a bullet, but had no control. He tried out for the major leagues, but couldn't get anyone to catch for him. So they hired his brother, who was used to him. A batter would dig in. The ball would go over the back stop. The batter would loosen up a bit; the next ball hit the dirt behind him. By the time Mizell was throwing strikes, the batter was four feet away from the batter's box.

Big Bend, as I called him, was elected to Congress in 1968. He had enjoyed a great career as a ballplayer and also as a substitute preacher who frequently filled the church. When he ran for Congress, his regular preacher announced that since Wilmer Mizell was preaching this Sunday, his political opponent had requested equal time and would be at the pulpit the following Sunday.

Wilmer, with his "aw, shucks" attitude, started, "As you know, I have been speaking on behalf of our Christ and Savior for many years. Next week my opponent will be here to speak for the opposition."

Nixon Gets the Bird

Every year the National Turkey Federation presents a large live bird to the president at Thanksgiving. One year, the head of the federation was David Graham from my district in Indiana. David brought the bird in a big cage. He had an employee to handle the heavy work.

The presentation was held in the Rose Garden at the White House. Secretary of Agriculture Clifford Harden was there. Congressman John Myers and I represented the Indiana delegation, and a photographer was there as usual to record the event for posterity. When President Nixon came out to get the bird, the handler took it out of the cage and sat it on top for the "photo opportunity."

Well, when the flash went off, the turkey took off, too. It ran around the Rose Garden at top speed, followed by the poor guy who was supposed to take care of it. When he finally caught the bird, he took off his belt to tie him down. As he carried the woebegone bird back to the cage, his pants fell down. Nixon laughed so hard he had to sit on some steps to recover.

Lake Woof Woof

In the early seventies, a group of people in Southern Illinois started a youth camp called Andessonk, supposedly an Indian name. It was a summer camp that was supported by the Catholic diocese.

In order to complete all the facilities for outdoor recreation, they needed a lake. Roy Ryan, an Evansville contractor and friend of mine, was asked to build it for them. Roy was a great humanitarian; he agreed to do it, and did.

When the lake was finished, Roy was asked to make the dedication address. Not one who enjoyed public speaking, he declined, suggesting instead that I (who loved public speaking) would be pleased to do so.

On the day of the special event, my wife Marge and I drove over to Carbondale, Illinois, to visit our daughter, who was a student at Southern Illinois University. Then we proceeded to drive down to Andessonk.

Unfortunately, we got lost and were a little late getting to the site. When we did get there, a large crowd had assembled, and the Bishop was addressing the audience from a special platform set up by the lake.

We were escorted through the crowd, and I was rushed up to the platform. Marge sat with some other women on a bench near the front of the audience.

The Bishop said some nice things about Ryan and then introduced me to "name and dedicate the lake." Now I had no idea what the lake was named and the Bishop had retreated to the audience and left me standing with a big crowd in front of me and the lake behind.

I tried to tell a few funny stories, stalled a bit, but finally had to face the fact that I was to name the lake.

With great gestures, I announced that it was my pleasure to dedicate Lake.... I turned away from the microphone, faced the lake and mumbled "woof woof."

Everyone applauded. The woman sitting next to Marge asked, "What did he say the name was?"

"I didn't hear," Marge responded.

Another woman said, "I think he said it was Lake Woof Woof."

You know, I still don't know what it's called.

Dynamite John

In the sixties, the Olinger Construction Company of Huntingburg, Indiana, had a contract to build part of U.S. 41 in Southern Indiana. They were a non-union company, which upset John Souci, head of the laborer's union. John called Lee Ray Olinger and threatened dire results if his men didn't join the union. Olinger refused.

A few nights later, Olinger's heavy road-building equipment was blown up with dynamite. After buying new equipment the three Olinger boys took turns standing guard with shotguns at night. The dynamiters didn't return.

Once "Dynamite John" — as he liked to be called — phoned me. "Some friends of yours are building a bank at Hatfield," he told me. "They aren't using my men. Now you know what happens when I get mad," he warned. "You'd better call them."

"Sorry, Dynamite," I answered. "I'm not in labor relations. I'm a federal legislator," I added, and hung up. In a couple of days, the bank was destroyed. The same thing happened to an apartment complex in downtown Evansville.

Though everyone suspected who did it, Souci was never charged.

Our son, Scott, had a summer job working on a highway project where Souci's men had a contract. Scott and his football buddies had to pay a fee to the union in order to get the job. One day they were "rip-rapping" an area near a bridge — taking large rocks from a pile and laying them along the bank of the road to prevent erosion.

Scott figured out how to use a sort of relay system where the boys would throw the rocks at each other. It was fun and gave them a lot of exercise, but it finished the job in one day when it was scheduled to take most of a week.

Dynamite John drove up. The boys were very proud of themselves and showed him their handiwork. He had them fired.

Scott and his buddies didn't like the idea of paying the union anyway, so they started a house-painting business which kept them busy for the rest of the summer.

Dynamite John didn't like me because his people had invested heavily in my opponent who bragged: "The unions pay for my campaigns and I never let them down."

After I was elected the first time, he came to see me in Washington. He and several of his very large associates barged into my office without pausing at the receptionist's desk.

"Dees is our demands," he announced, and handed me a list of union legislative goals.

"Now, Dynamite," I responded. "You did everything you could to keep me from being elected. Why should I help you?"

"You is right, I did." Souci replied. "Do as we want, and we'll work just as hard for you next time."

Sure he would.

Great Dane Remembers

Andrew Jacobs Jr. of Indiana was elected to Congress in 1964. He is a totally charming and witty fellow, but some folks may say he is a bit eccentric.

Andy, a Democrat, has been known to take the microphone in the well of the House and utter a single word like, "Oh?" or "Why?"

Back in the early 1970's, Andy was opposed to a large cargo plane (the C-5)) which the Air Force planned to acquire. About the same time Andy got a Great Dane dog, which he named "C-5." Where most members of Congress have large government-supplied desks and chairs, Andy worked on a card table in one corner of his office. He had a little, indoor garden, complete with waterfall and fish tank for C-5. Staff people took the dog out for walks at regular intervals.

One day Congressman James W. Symington of Missouri, a fellow Democrat, was walking down the hall outside Andy's door. C-5 got a whiff of him, ran out the door, and bit him rather severely on the hand. It was a totally unprovoked attack and surprised everyone.

In the 1971 election, Andy was defeated by William H. Hudnut, who later became mayor of Indianapolis. Andy went home and took C-5 with him.

The year 1974 was bad for Republicans, thanks to Watergate. Hudnut was defeated and Andy was re-elected. He didn't bring C-5 back with him right away, but after a few months, the dog returned to the office garden.

Symington heard that C-5 was back so he brought him a peace offering of some cheese. At first C-5 happily ate the cheese. Then he sniffed Symington and bit him again.

Bella the Bull

When Bella Abzug was elected in 1970, she created quite a ripple. She was anything but delicate in appearance, and had a personality that matched. Tales of Bella's exploits ran rampant. I presume that most of them were true.

Several observers were on the House floor when she first visited it and met "Fishbait" Miller, the House doorkeeper. They say that "Fishbait" told her that she couldn't come to the floor in one of her famous hats. Anyone in the vicinity could hear her ask, "How long do you have to be in this @#$* institution before you can tell this @#$* to go @#$* himself?"

With this introduction to Congress, her fame spread rapidly. She allied herself with Jane Fonda, Ramsey Clark and other anti-war activists. It was said that some of her staff people set up housekeeping in her office.

I served on the Public Works Committee with Bella but she seldom showed up for meetings. That is, she seldom showed up until they started televising the proceedings. Then she arrived with bells on, or rather with a hat on, and was most conspicuous.

The committee had an occasional party to celebrate some event or other. If there was music, Bella and staff director Dick Sullivan entertained by dancing together to "Sidewalks of New York." For a couple of big people, they were remarkably agile.

Bella demanded attention wherever she went and occupied center stage. Her husband, Martin (the poor soul), was never heard to say a word. Once, on an oversees "fact-finding mission," the congressional delegation was entertained at a cocktail party and dinner.

Bella, as usual, was expounding on some subject *ad nauseam* and Martin was his usual quiet self. Members who attended the party say that Martin uttered the only words that had ever come out of his mouth. Maybe the cocktails and maybe the years of frustration caused him to say, "Bella, shut up!"

No one seems to remember what happened after that.

Whoops, Wrong Congressman

Lyndon Johnson invited groups of congressmen to the White House in 1967 to explain his policy on the Vietnam War. One such meeting nearly caused me to miss my flight home for the weekend.

The meeting was in the President's conference room on a Friday afternoon, and I knew I was going to have a tough time making it to the airport in time. As I left the White House, I asked a staffer to please call Eastern Air Lines and have an employee meet me at the entrance so I wouldn't have to look up the gate. Representative John Myers, also of Indiana, attended the briefing and agreed to drive me to the airport. I'm glad members of Congress are granted immunity from traffic fines because we moved along at a pretty good clip.

John dumped me at the entrance to the airport and I rushed in, expecting to be met. No one was there, so I looked up the gate and ran down to try to catch the plane.

When I got to the gate the plane was gone. "Hey!" I complained, "Someone was supposed to meet me."

"Who are you?" I was asked.

"Congressman Zion," I replied.

"Oh God," the man at the gate gasped, "I must have put the wrong man on." He called the plane captain, who returned the plane the gate.

What had happened was that Congressman Bill Stuckey of the famous Stuckey roadside stops in Georgia was rushing to make a plane to Atlanta. As he ran into the airport entrance my anticipated guide asked, "Congressman?"

"Yes," Stuckey replied, wondering why someone was meeting him.

"Follow me," she said and led him down to the gate. Well, I got to make my connection in Louisville, but Bill had to catch a plane three hours later.

The Sorority House

Floyd Spence of South Carolina was elected in 1968 and moved into the Coronet Apartments, just three blocks east of the House Office Buildings. The Coronet was run by some busybodies who stuck their noses into everyone's business. They put notes in your mailbox if they suspected any hanky-panky.

On his first morning in Congress, Floyd got on the elevator and started down. It stopped at the next floor and a young woman got on. Floyd said, "Hi," and they proceeded to the lobby floor. As they left the front door of the apartment, Floyd, being a Southern gentleman, opened the door for her. He went his way and she went hers.

About that time, the young lady's fiancee called the desk to ask about her. "She went out with Floyd Spence this morning," he was told.

"Who is Floyd Spence?" he shouted.

"He's a new Congressman from South Carolina."

By the time Floyd got to his office, he had an irate caller who demanded to know what Floyd was doing with his girl. As soon as Floyd calmed down, he went to the Coronet and checked out.

Bush: Man of the Year

The one place in Washington that makes sense is the House gym. Members of all shapes, sizes and political persuasions get together and engage in vigorous games of basketball or paddleball, or just work out. They can return to their committees, correspondence, telephone, etc., with renewed energy after a good workout.

One year the gym committee decided to honor a "Man of the Year" at an annual gym banquet. Morris Udall of Utah was selected. Mo was a great chairman of the Interior Committee, but was best known for his sense of humor. At the appropriate time, the chairman of the gym committee introduced Mo, and he came forward to accept his award. We were all ready. As arranged, we started pelting him with rolls, knotted napkins, ice cubes, and anything else that would serve as a missile. Grabbing a large serving tray, Mo ducked behind it and avoided most of the debris. It was all done in good humor, we had a great time, and we enjoyed the evening.

The next year, Vice President George Bush was selected. He had all the required Secret Service men, plus the Capitol Police (campus cops) standing around the room. As Bush got up to receive his award, he quickly explained, "if any of you guys are planning to give me the Mo Udall treatment, you'd better forget it. Those guys with the hearing aids all have itchy trigger fingers."

It was said in jest, of course, but as I looked around every member was sitting with hands on the table.

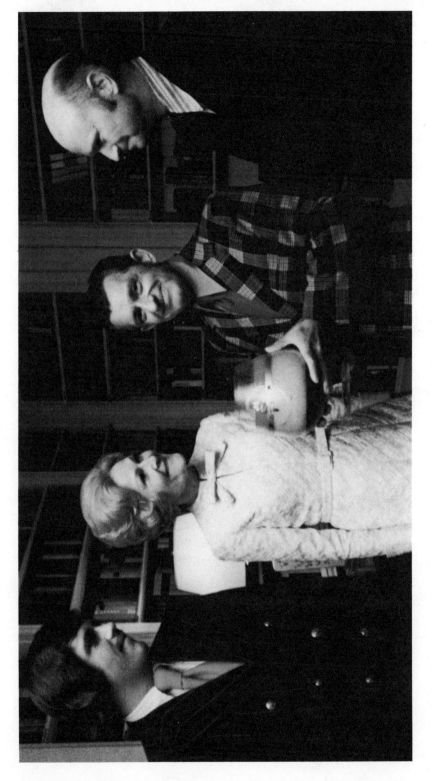

First Lady Pat Nixon brightens the day by lighting a red, white, and blue candle being held by the man who made it, a constituent of mine. He thought it would be a great idea to have the First Lady light the candle for Evansville's freedom festival celebration one year.

45

Out, Out Brief Candle

Evansville has a freedom festival celebration every Fourth of July. It is a big affair with lots of hype and enthusiasm.

In 1970, a candlemaker thought it would be great if we had a big flame and that it should lighted by the first lady, Pat Nixon. He called me and asked if I could arrange it. Mrs. Nixon was delighted to accommodate us, and we set a date.

The candle maker made a thick candle with red, white and blue wax. He took the back seat out of his car, fixed a wind-proof shield for the candle, and started for Washington. I met him in front of my office building, and we drove to the White House. We met the First Lady in a reception room. She had been briefed, of course, but wanted to strike up a conversation with the candle maker. "What can I do for you?" she asked.

Nothing. Not a peep came from him.

"Where are you from?" she asked. He couldn't answer that either. I have never seen anyone so completely tongue-tied before. Finally, she acknowledged that she was pleased to light his candle, did so with a flourish, and asked him if she could show him around the White House.

He still didn't answer but handed me the candle and went off with Pat Nixon.

I had called my office and asked for someone to pick me up at the East Wing of the White House so I could get back to work.

Now, I have never told anyone this story before, so promise you'll never, never tell a single soul. This is our secret. As I took the candle out to the car, it blew out.

I was late for a meeting, Mrs. Nixon was off somewhere being a tour guide, and I didn't know what to do. So, I did the only brave thing I could do: head for the office.

When I arrived at the office I grabbed an elevator and headed up. Several people looked at me, then the candle, then back to me again. "Got a light?" I asked. Some guy fumbled for a lighter, lit my candle, and put me back in business.

Later the candle maker came for his "pride and joy," and drove it all the way back to Indiana. I've never told anyone about this, but maybe the statute of limitations has run out and I won't be crucified for my carelessness.

You know, I'm wondering. Do you think that guy really got that thing all the way back to Indiana without it going out? Maybe someday he will have a story to tell.

Elephant Equestrian Extraordinaire

In 1973, Karen Feld, whose family owns the Ringling Brothers and Barnum and Bailey Circus, called me. "How about riding an elephant on opening day at the circus?" she asked.

"Not me," I told her with some appropriate emphasis.

"Oh, that's too bad," she sighed. "Bob Michel and Tom Railsback are riding."

Well, that did it. Bob and Tom, two of my buddies from Illinois, weren't going to show me up.

At the appointed time I arrived at the arena. Karen was there, Representative Dan Flood of Pennsylvania was there, five huge elephants were there, but no Michel or Railsback. I still don't know whether they chickened out or never intended to come in the first place.

Anyway, Flood had a big bunch of carrots. "If I'm going to ride this beast, I'm going to bribe him first." Dan told me. "Give me some of those," I begged.

For some reason I was assigned the lead elephant. A monster. The trainer had him kneel down so I could get on. After scrambling up on his knee, I grabbed his halter, and about that time he stood up. I thought I was going into orbit. I held the halter with one hand and those dumb carrots in the other and he took off. It was a terrifying experience. Elephants are very tall.Later, Karen sent me a very beautiful certificate naming me to the Royal Order of Pachyderms. It is framed and hangs in a prominent place in my Washington apartment.

RINGLING BROS. AND BARNUM & BAILEY CIRCUS

WHEREAS

Hon. Roger Zion of Evansville, Indiana

has perfectly performed perched
precariously on a Ponderous Pachyderm
of THE GREATEST SHOW ON EARTH and,
WHEREAS, this ride was carried through with
disciplined dignity and absolute aplomb, Therefore,
RINGLING BROS. AND BARNUM & BAILEY CIRCUS
hereby confers upon the above-named Regal Rider
the celebrated and coveted title

ELEPHANT EQUESTRIAN EXTRAORDINAIRE

Presented in Washington, D.C.

on this 5th day of April, A.D. 19 73

Karen Feld
Engagement Director

Jim Feld
President
Ringling Bros. and Barnum & Bailey Combined Shows, Inc.

I'm famous at last, as this proclamation from Ringling Bros. and Barnum and Bailey Circus proves. Now I can list among my many public achievements, "Elephant Equestrian Extraordinaire."

Joe Garagiola and astronaut Harrison Schmitt sit on either side of me as we attend ceremonies in honor of fallen astronaut Gus Grissom. Schimtt was a great astronaut, but obviously uncomfortable with public speaking, in contrast to the gregarious Joe.

Joe Garagiola inspects a space capsule in Mitchell, Indiana, hometown of Virgil "Gus" Grissom. Grissom was killed in the 1967 Apollo accident, and we were invited to help dedicate a memorial to him.

Joe Garagiola and Gin

After the tragedy that ended the lives of Apollo astronauts Ed White, Roger Chaffee, and Virgil "Gus" Grissom in January 1967, I was asked to go with Joe Garagiola to dedicate a memorial to Gus at his hometown of Mitchell, Indiana. Joe was working as a commentator with "The Today Show" at the time.

A private plane picked me up in Washington and flew to New York to get Joe. When we got to the airport he wasn't there. We called his office and found that he was waiting at another airport. Well, you can't just hop from one New York airport to another. You must get altitude, enter a pattern and let down at your alternate destination.

By the time we did all that, it was apparent that we would be late for the ceremony. When the inevitable arrives, you just make the most of it. The co-pilot brought us a deck of cards and we started to play gin rummy. While we were playing, I couldn't help but show resentment over the way "The Today Show" was treating the Vietnam War. I asked Joe why only ultra-liberal, left-wing extremists were interviewed on the subject. "Don't tell me you're one of those?" I asked.

"Hell, no!" Joe assured me. "I'm the most conservative wop you'll ever see."

"Why do you sit still and let those guys dictate the philosophy of the show then?" I asked.

"Do you know how much they are paying me?" Joe replied.

We landed too late for the ceremony but in time for a dinner that was scheduled after the dedication. I got beat pretty bad at the gin game, which shows that it's strictly a game of luck. Skill has nothing to do with it. Joe autographed the scorecard: "Congressman— For the first time the government paid me! It was a pleasure."

Dick and Ed

Ed Mitchell was a one-term Congressman from my district in Southern Indiana. He had been a Navy frogman during World War II and was a real tough cookie. He was elected at the same time as Richard Nixon, and the two had adjoining offices in the Cannon

Richard Nixon remains a mystery—sometimes ill at ease with others but always faithful to his friends.

House Office Building and shared a secretary. Her name was Rose-mary Woods, and she became famous because of some missing conversation on the Watergate tapes.

Ed was very fond of Dick Nixon and handled his presidential campaigns in Indiana in 1968 and 1972.

Whenever I saw President Nixon he asked me about Ed, and I always gave him the latest scoop. Once I was happy to tell him that Ed had encountered a former political foe at the McCurdy Hotel in Evansville. After a few unpleasantries, Ed decked the guy with one punch.

Later, some American ambassador was kidnapped and locked in the trunk of a car. Nixon came up to me at a reception and commented, "If ol' Mitchell had been our ambassador, those kidnappers would have had a real tiger in their tank."

The Quarterback Club

A group of bigwigs get together each year in Washington to honor some top athletes. They call themselves the Quarterback Club. After a long cocktail hour, they have an endless banquet with more drinking and lots of speeches.

You may recall that in 1988, John Riggins, star running back for the Redskins, was sitting next to U.S. Supreme Court Justice Sandra Day O'Connor at the annual banquet when he slid to the floor and told her to "Lighten up, Baby."

So you can see that the atmosphere at these things is somewhat cloudy.

Anyway, back in the second Nixon Administration, Ed was a guest at the Quarterback Club and wound up at the same table as Hale Boggs, the Democratic leader of the House.

During dinner Boggs made some uncomplimentary comments about Ed's pal, Dick Nixon. When Boggs got up to go to the men's room, Ed followed him. A short time later Ed returned to the table alone.

Poor Boggs was out cold on the men's room floor.

The next day I got a call from a reporter with *The Washington*

Post. I wasn't in the office, so my legislative assistant answered for me. "Does the Congressman know Ed Mitchell?" the reporter asked.

"Why, what has he done now?" my assistant asked.

"He decked Hale Boggs at a banquet," the reporter responded.

"Mitchell is one of the Congressman's best friends," he was told.

The Thirty-Hour Session

In October of 1968, Representative Donald Rumsfeld of Illinois decided to show how obsolete the Rules of the House were. ("Rummy" later became White House chief of staff, ambassador to the United Nations, president of the Searle Company and candidate for president.) He recruited California Representative Bob Mathias and me to help him. We found an antique car and had our picture taken in front of it with a caption saying that the House rules were as old as the car and about as useful.

The House went into session at noon on a Tuesday. The usual procedure was to dispense with the minutes of Monday's session. We objected and asked that the total congressional record of the previous day's work be read. We didn't object to the minutes, but we called the reading in order to make our point.

Now, there is a lot more to the record than just what is said on the floor. Any member can ask unanimous consent that any statement of any length be published in the record. Frequently the added material is much longer than the statements that are made on any given day.In order to dispense with the reading, the House must be called together and vote to dispense. This takes time. Most members had more important things to do than sit on the floor and listen to the debate. We became rather unpopular by demanding a vote on every issue, and every procedure that came up. This was before we had an electronic voting system. The clerk had to call the roll beginning with Adair and Addabo; a half hour later, getting around to Zion and Zwach.

Well we kept this up all Tuesday and Tuesday night. Many members got tired of the delaying tactics and went home. The House can't adjourn unless the members vote to adjourn; without a quorum present to vote, we had to stay in session.

To pass the time, Del Clawson of California brought his saxophone over and played accompaniment for Charlotte Reed of Illinois, who sang a few numbers from the House balcony.

Though there was no one outside to hear her, if there had been, they would have enjoyed it. Before being elected to Congress, Charlotte was a vocalist on Don McNeal's radio breakfast club in Chicago.

About two in the morning, Speaker John McCormack ordered that the doors be locked and that a warrant be issued for the arrest of members not present. Zeake Johnson, Sergeant at Arms, was required to bring in all members who weren't on the floor. Every now and then a sleepy-eyed member would show up, but we didn't have a quorum to vote to close up shop.

Members were sleeping on the floor, in the cloak room, in their seats, and anywhere else that offered serenity.

About three in the morning, Bob Taft, a large member from Ohio, burst out of the chamber through the door behind the Speaker's chair. Zeake Johnson was close behind him. Zeake was about half as big as Taft and we all speculated about whether Zeake would bring him back.

After about one minute, Taft came back through the door and approached the microphone in the well of the House. "Mr. Speaker," he announced, "My prerogatives preceded those of the House." We all had a good laugh, realizing that Bob Taft Jr., of the famous Taft family, had the temerity to visit the men's room against the Speaker's orders.

We kept up the delaying tactics until the Speaker and Majority Leader agreed to review the Rules of the House with the objective of finding ways to modernize. We finished business about 8:30 p.m. on Wednesday, ending the longest session of the House in history.

Hallowed Howls

While the indiscretions of our lawmakers are well publicized, our congressmen are primarily human beings who suffer from the same foibles and enjoy the same pleasures as the constituents they represent. If they didn't have a sense of humor, they would explode.

Back in the days of the Wilbur Mills-Fanne Foxe-Tidal Basin episode, it was popular to make up funny stories about what really went on that fateful night. Congressman Mills and Foxe, a stripper, were returning from a drinking party when a police car pulled them over for weaving back and forth. Foxe (in no condition to be rational) tried to escape, only to run right into the tidal basin. The incident made the national news and was a subject of conversation for weeks.

To hear the latest fable, you merely had to go to the Democratic or Republican cloakrooms where the real wit and wisdom of the Congress is expressed. The cloakrooms are two narrow rooms adjoining the House floor. They are lined with chairs, divans and telephones where members can relax, have a smoke or a sandwich, and exchange ribald stories. It usually takes about one day for a rumor to transcend both houses of Congress and both sides of the aisle.

The day after the tidal basin fiasco, the big question was, "Did you know that Carl Albert was in Wilbur's car last night but didn't get caught?" Carl Albert, then-Speaker of the House, hailed from Bug Tussle, Oklahoma. Not only did he come from a tiny town, but he was also one of the smallest men to serve in either house of Congress.

"Yeah, how come?"

"He hid in the glove compartment."

Sam Steiger of Arizona was one of the more colorful characters of the House. When he held forth in the cloakroom, it was hard to find an empty chair.

He tells a story about taking a friend hunting on an Arizona farm. The farmer had agreed to let them hunt, but asked Sam as a favor to shoot an old mule that was in bad shape and wouldn't survive the winter.

Trying to be funny, Sam told his friend that the farmer was an ornery ol' cuss and wasn't going to let them hunt.

"I'm so mad I'm going to shoot the first animal I see," Sam threatened (he had just caught sight of the sick old mule). With that, he walked through the woods and plugged the mule between the eyes.

He was chuckling as he returned to the Jeep until he heard a loud bang from the other side of the road. "Run," his friend yelled, "I just shot his prize bull!"

When Sam was first elected to Congress, he was invited to appear on the Joe Pine Show. Pine was a sensationalist who liked to shock his audience.

He took Sam to dinner and plied him with booze just before the broadcast. As the program progressed, Sam suggested that some Members of Congress drank to excess and others were too stupid to wheel a wheelbarrow. In general, the program was the kind that made Pine famous, but didn't do much to enhance the image of Congress.

A couple of days later, Sam and I were playing paddleball in the House gym. The thong on my paddle broke, and the paddle slipped out of my hand and broke Sam's nose.

One of Washington's newsmen explained it this way: "They take care of their own. When Sam Steiger, freshman Congressman from Arizona, dared to criticize his fellow members, Congressman Zion, ex-Navy strongman, broke his nose."

When I heard about it, I almost died. Fortunately Sam didn't believe a word of the accusation and permitted me to live.

Sam Steiger also tells a story about his wife's first hunting expedition. He had bought a rifle for her, taught her to shoot, and outfitted her with all the appropriate equipment for deer-hunting in the Arizona hills.

"One thing you must remember, though," he told her, "is that there are more hunters than deer out here. If you shoot one, you have to be very fast or some other hunter will steal the carcass before you can say scat."

"Don't worry, honey," she replied, "if I hit one, we are going to keep it."

Late one afternoon, Sam heard a rifle crack near where his wife was hunting. He rushed through the woods to see her holding her gun right under the nose of a cowboy. He had his hands in the air and was gasping.

"Yes ma'am, that's your buck and you can have him, but can I take my saddle off of him first?"

Sam is Snowed

John Rhodes of Arizona, ex-Minority Leader, told of going hunting with Sam up in the mountains one winter. It seems their jeep bogged down in the snow and wouldn't move. The only thing they could do was mush up to a lodge that was closed for the winter. After banging on the door for a while, the widow who owned the place peeked out. Seeing that they were harmless, she let them in.

She cooked them a nice dinner and they sat by the fire, then went down the hall to a guest room. The next day, a trapper with a team of horses pulled them out of the snow and they went on their way.

Exactly nine months later John called Sam and demanded, "Meet me in the cloakroom right away." Sam rushed over to find that John was excited. "Do you remember nine months ago when we were stranded in that mountain lodge?"

"Yes I do," Sam admitted.

"Did you go down the hall and visit that widow lady? And by any chance did you tell her that you were Congressman John Rhodes?" Sam weakly nodded in the affirmative.

"Well, Sam I want you to know..... that she died and left me the lodge."

Endangered Species

Sam likes to tell of a hunting trip that John went on with a Boy Scout troop.

They were cooking their evening meal when a game warden interrupted them. "What is that you're cooking?" he asked. "I really don't know," John responded.

"Why it's a condor! An endangered species." gasped the game warden. "I'll see you in court tomorrow morning."

So the next morning found John and his scouts in front of a federal judge. "You don't understand, Judge," John explained. "Our canoe turned over. We lost all our supplies. If we hadn't eaten that condor we would have starved to death."

The judge thought a while and finally decided to drop the

charges. As the scouts were leaving the courtroom, he asked, "What in the world does a condor taste like?"

One of the scouts offered an answer. "Well, judge," the boy explained, "It tastes like a cross between a whooping crane and a bald eagle."

Flight of Terror

If you visit your nation's capital these days and are privileged to watch the antics of the House of Representatives from the visitors' gallery, you are first subjected to a metallic scanner that prevents you from taking guns, grenades, or other potential weapons along with you.

The scanners were first used in 1976, despite the fact that would-be assassins had gained access to the gallery earlier.

Back in the early 1960s, for example, before I was elected to the House, five Puerto Ricans opened fire at the Members on the floor from a public balcony behind the Speaker's desk. Several Members were painfully, but not fatally, wounded in the attack.

One rather short, heavy member from Alabama, Frank Boyken, started running at the first shot. As he rushed down the east front stairs of the Capitol, a colleague asked, "Where are you going, Frank?

"To get my gun," the fleeing member responded.

"Where is it?" he was asked.

"Alabama!" was the answer.

Congressional Test Drivers

Around 1970, a group of members of the Public Works Committee was invited to visit the General Motors Proving Grounds in Detroit.

The GM people wanted to show us their safety suggestions and mobilize us against the catalytic converter that was being proposed by some members of Congress at the time.

It was a very enlightening experience from several points of view. Jack McDonald of Michigan and I were assigned to ride around the grounds to see some highway safety suggestions. We were in the back seat of a car when the driver turned around and started talking to us. His hands were off the wheel. Jack shouted and, I thought, was about to jump out of the car as it swerved toward a bridge.

As it got to the bridge, the car suddenly straightened out and went through with no help from the driver.

As we caught our breath, the driver explained that the road had been built with curbs that directed the car though the bridge even if the steering wheel was unattended. GM had a lot of good suggestions to prevent highway accidents.

Each of us got to try our skill at driving on wet pavement and through an obstacle course. New suspension systems were being tested.

Then we were assembled around a new car to see an invention with which we were not familiar. I was "volunteered" to be the tester.

The demonstrator asked me to sit in the front seat and pretend to be driving down the road. "Let's pretend you suddenly hit a tree," he suggested. Wham! I thought I was shot.

A large fabric balloon suddenly started inflating in front of me and pinned me to the seat.

We witnessed one of the first air bag restraints. In those days, the bag was inflated by a regular, ten-gauge shotgun shell. It scared the bejabbers out of me.

Future Speaker in Danger

Because of predicted long-range oil shortages, auto manufacturers were experimenting with battery-operated cars. GM had a prototype and was anxious for us to see it.

Jim Wright of Texas and I were asked to give it a test drive. Jim thought I should drive, and he hopped into the passenger side. The car was pretty small and I remember asking if you got into it or put it on.

After adjusting the seatbelts Jim yelled, "Contact!" and I pushed down on the accelerator. The car lurched across the road and right into the path of an approaching truck. Superior evasive maneuvers by the truck driver prevented us from being smashed like a couple of bugs.

As we breathlessly returned to our hosts and "took off" the little car, we found a bunch of red faces. The GM executives had ordered the road closed to all traffic during our test drive. Somehow the truck driver didn't get the word. I wondered what the party responsible for the mix-up is now doing for a job.

Never on a Monday and Sabotage in the Plant

At a dinner party that concluded our visit, I was seated next to GM's vice president of production. I had heard that cars assembled on a Monday or Friday were more likely to have defects than those built on a Tuesday through Thursday, and I asked him if that was true.

He confirmed that it was. Apparently workers came to work on Monday either hung-over or tired from the weekend activities. They find it difficult to get back in the swing of their work. On Friday, they are members of the "T.G.I.F. group," and are looking forward to a fun weekend.

I told the production manager that I had ordered a Grand Prix and asked if he could assure me that it wasn't built on a Monday or Friday.

"When you get back home, call your Pontiac dealer and get the purchase order number of your car. I'll try to personally supervise it as it goes through the assembly process. I just hope the workers don't sabotage it for you without my notice."

"What do you mean 'sabotage'?" I asked. He told me that if the autoworkers suspect a VIP car is in the works, they purposely leave out a few bolts or slip a coke bottle into the paneling so that it rattles. "There are lots of little things they can do to mess up a car. They think it's a lot of fun." he responded.

When my car arrived and I took delivery, I was suspicious. Actually it was the best car I've ever had. I guess the boss got by with that one.

Chapter Three

Members of Congress have one thing in common. They have been introduced to speak at countless banquets, rallies, dedications, and meetings of all kinds. Some of the introductions are embarrassing because of undue flattery and some are just the opposite.

A moderately flattering introduction for me was once concluded with, "And now we hear the latest dope from Washington—the Honorable Roger Zion."

A friend of mine was handed a note from his wife just before he mounted a podium for an important speech. I was sitting next to him and couldn't help see what it said—just the word KISS in bold capital letters.

I thought this was a sweet gesture by his help-mate and couldn't understand why he gave her a mild scowl before his remarks. Later I learned what she meant. She had listened to too many political speeches in her day. The note, KISS, was an admonition to "Keep It Simple, Stupid."

Vietnam War Protesters

During the Vietnam War, the nation's capitol was full of protesters. Students from Yale descended on us *en masse* with a message from their president that we must protest the war. We were asked to wear anti-war buttons. Many of us tried to explain that we were against war too, but that we couldn't tolerate having strong nations subjugate weak ones.

A group of long-haired, especially disreputable looking "peaceniks" were picketing the Coronet apartments one morning, knowing that several congressmen were living there. Bill Bray, of Indiana, a former World War II tank commander, looked out the window and saw them. He called Representative Dick Roudebush (later Veterans Administration head) and me, and told us about it, since we both lived there, too, and were in our rooms.

"What should we do?" I asked.

"I don't know about you guys," Bill answered, "but as for me, I'm calling the press. I want them to record what kind of people are working against me."

After the TV cameras arrived, we walked out of the front door of the apartment building to the jeers of the picketers. "If you don't sign our petition," we were told, "we will come out to Indiana and campaign against you."

"If you promise to do that," Bray told them, "I'll pay your expenses."

In 1968, some students at Indiana University challenged the congressional delegation to come to Bloomington to debate the merits of the war. Most of us were too busy in our own districts and didn't accept the invitation.

The students were offended and made a big case of it. The press was unkind to us for shirking our responsibility and they, too, gave us a bad time. A group of my constituents joined in chastising me.

The next year, I decided to drive up to Bloomington and "face the music." As I recall, there were five Congressmen who showed up: Lee Hamilton, Andy Jacobs, John Myers, Bill Bray and me. After all the hoopla from the students, few came to the meeting.

I doubt if there were more than thirty students out of an enrollment of thousands.

Only one of them was from my district. He was a campaigner for my opponent. The few students who came did so to "give us hell." They railed on about the evils of war and the terrible effects of disrupting their education etc., etc. Then they turned on Bill Bray, a senior member of the Armed Services Committee, and really gave him a working over. Bill explained that he, too, was very much opposed to war and wished that these students would contact the North Vietnamese and Viet Cong and talk them out of waging war on the innocent people of South Vietnam. Bill tried to tell them that the only way to stop war is to make it unprofitable for the war mongers. He didn't buy the students' argument that if the U.S. unilaterally destroyed all its weapons, the rest of the world would follow suit.

After about an hour, John Myers and I decided that we weren't going to convince the students to back our military activities, so we ducked out. The ex-tank commander, "Wild Bill" Bray, stayed and argued with them for another hour. I think all people involved would agree that the confrontation was an exercise in futility.

A month later, a group of officials from Indiana University had a dinner reception for the congressional delegation in Washington. They wanted us to help them gain additional funding for the school.

IU was considered one of the more liberal universities at the time and didn't clamp down on some pretty excessive student activities After the officials gave their pitch, Bill Bray got up and announced, "You guys are going to have to decide who runs that school, you or the students. If you turn it over to the students, I'll see that you don't get a thin dime." Myers and I agreed with him.

I don't recall that there was any significant tightening up of the reins at Bloomington, but we gave it our best shot.

Bray was defeated in 1974 with the big "Watergate Baby" election. I saw him a couple of times after that and he always had an interesting story to tell. Once, he was walking down the street and met a former constituent. "Hello, Mr. Bray," she greeted him. "You remember me, don't you?"

"No, madam, I do not," he responded. He hadn't been able to admit that for sixteen years, and took great pleasure in it.

The 300-Pound Cop

One day in the early 1970s, my staff got a call from the Republican Whip office telling us to drop by the House Cloak Room to see some pictures that were taken in Laos. U.S. military forces had crossed into Laos to seize a large cache of weapons that were being used against our fighting men in Vietnam.

There was a large hue and cry from some people, protesting the "extension of the war into Laos." Many Congressmen joined in condemning President Nixon for approving it.

I looked at the pictures. There were thousands of rifles, huge stacks of ammunition, and mountains of bombs that had been captured. I asked for copies of the pictures and headed for the House recording studio, where I could make tapes to share with my constituents.

Just as I got to Independence Avenue, a gang of anti-war protesters accosted me. They asked me what I was doing with the pictures. I told them that this was evidence that our military leaders were wise to cross over into Laos. "These pictures prove that this incursion probably saved hundreds of American lives." I told them.

With that, the students tried to grab the pictures out of my hand. We had a real tug-of-war going. Then, all of a sudden, help appeared in the form of "Tiny." Tiny was a 300-pound ex-football tackle who escorted members of Congress across the street and maintained order at the corner of South Capitol and Independence avenues. "Having a problem, Mr. Zion?" he asked. The students scattered like a Fourth of July fireworks burst.

"Not now I'm not," I told him.

Starvation Wages

Early in 1970, Representative Larry Winn of Kansas came over to me on the House floor and asked if I would speak at a fundraiser for him in Kansas City. "When?" I asked.

"Tonight," he answered.

Senator Bob Packwood of Oregon had agreed to speak but backed out at the last minute when he found out that he would be traveling in a private plane. Representative Bob Price of Texas was sitting next to me. "Let's both go," I suggested. "I'll warm up the crowd with a bunch of tales and you can give 'em a real fire and brimstone sermon on why we should support our President and his determination to liberate the South Vietnamese."

"Great," agreed Price. Bob had been a jet fighter pilot during the Korean War and could speak with authority. Winn's wife, Joan, picked us up at the bottom of the Capitol steps and drove us to the airport. I had missed lunch because of an important committee meeting, and was pretty hungry. All we had in the provision locker of the plane was a can of peanuts and a bottle of scotch. By the time these items were shared by the four of us, no one's appetite was curbed.

We were an hour late getting to the Kansas City airport, and a police car was waiting to escort us to the auditorium. I remember rushing along a country road with the siren screaming.

As we overtook an old car with an elderly man at the wheel, he became excited and took off into a cornfield. By the time we got to the meeting place, the crowd of a couple thousand people had eaten dinner and were milling around waiting for Senator Packwood to give the address. When they heard the siren, they assembled in the auditorium.

Congressman Winn was introduced. He explained that Bob Packwood was unable to attend at the last minute, and introduced me to introduce Price. I went through one of my comedy routines and then introduced the Korean War hero, the gentleman from Texas, the Honorable Bob Price.

Packwood was recognized as a "dove" at a time when Americans were classified as "hawks" or "doves," depending on whether they supported our effort in Vietnam or not. Price was a hawk. Instead of hearing the expected soft-on-the-war speech from Packwood, Price gave them a real drum-rolling, tub-thumping, hand-clapping, flag- waving, pro-involvement speech. He sat down to a thunderous ovation.

There was supposed to have been a cocktail reception before the dinner, where the guests who paid extra could meet and shake hands with Packwood and Winn. Since we were late, they scheduled the reception for after the meeting.

As is the usual procedure, the speakers stood in line as the guests filed past and exchanged pleasantries. For some reason, the hosts of the event felt that the hard-working speakers needed liquid refreshment. They kept sneaking up behind us and giving us cocktails.

That was the last thing we needed. I would gladly have traded a case of scotch for a hot dog or some potato chips. When all the guests had given us the benefit of their wisdom, it was late at night. Joan and Larry tried to find a place to eat. Nothing was open.

They took us to the hotel. I was assigned a suite that was reserved for Packwood, and was sure there would be a bowl of fruit on the table. Was there? No — just a bottle of scotch. Ugh! Early the next morning I was awakened. I didn't feel good at all, but I dressed and went down to breakfast. Bob Price was already in the dining room. Just as I arrived, his usual Texas breakfast of steak and eggs was served. I took one look and retired to the hotel lobby.

Somehow, after starving for so long, the picture of Bob's harvest breakfast almost did me in. Just before our plane left for Washington, I managed to eat a bowl of oatmeal. Now I know what people mean when they say they work for starvation wages.

Blush Blush Blush

One evening Winn and I and several other members were asked to attend a fundraiser for some cause at the Capitol Hill Club. Larry was quite an athlete in his early days, but he had a very unfortunate accident. He was pushing a boat out from shore one day when his brother started the motor. The prop sliced Larry almost in two and in the process cut off one of his legs. It was a miracle that he survived, but he did. He continued his interest in sports as a commentator on WHB radio in Kansas City. He then enjoyed a very successful career as a builder, civic leader and politician.

Who knows what he would have done if he hadn't had the accident.

Anyway, Larry and I were seated at a table when a young lady came up and asked Larry to dance. "Sorry," he said, "Thank you, but I don't dance."

"What's the matter?" the young lady asked, "You got a wooden leg?"

Larry didn't say a word. He just turned in his chair and went "thump, thump, thump" with his knuckles on his wooden leg. We caught her before she fell.

We Meet the Big Brass

It's amazing that so many of these stories start: "I was sitting on the House floor when...," but I guess that's where a lot of things do start. One evening during my first term, another freshman Congressman, Jack McDonald of Michigan, asked me if I would drive out to Fort Belvoir with him. Constituents frequently ask members of Congress to check up on military relatives, and the military is used to these visits. I said, "Sure."

Jack called his office and asked his secretary to call the base and tell them that he and Congressman Zion were coming out that evening to see Private Jerry Isbell.

The House was in session later that we expected, but we headed for Fort Belvoir as soon as we adjourned. When we arrived at the gate, we were met by a major, who saluted briskly and escorted us to the commanding general's quarters. The general was entertaining guests, but he left them to visit with us. He had a flip-chart presentation that detailed the mission of the fort. He gave a thorough explanation of the Army Engineers and just what Congress was getting for its buck when it backed the military budget, as far as his command was concerned.

Then he wondered why we wanted to see Private Isbell. He assumed that Jerry had issued a complaint and that Jack and I were there to investigate it. He had called Isbell's sergeant, lieutenant, captain and everyone down the line to see what caused the flap. They in turn called in the private and asked him what the beef was. The kid was scared stiff. "Oh, he's my wife's brother," Jack told the general. "We just came out to say hello and buy him a beer."

The general, colonel, captain, et al., exchanged glances and, I guess, felt rather silly. "Can we see Jerry?" Jack asked.

"Of course," the officers agreed as a chorus.

"Where can we get a beer?" Jack asked. "The officers' club," someone suggested. "Er...ah—the private can't go to the officers' club," we were told. "He can wear my sports coat and go as a civilian," one of the officers suggested. So we did. We drank a beer and fulfilled Jack's obligation to his wife, avoided a major confrontation and ended another day in the lives of two freshman congressmen.

No Bread

Once in the early 1970s, Secretary of Agriculture Earl Butz was negotiating with the Russians to buy a substantial amount of our excess wheat. Many millers and bakers were upset about the deal. They felt that by selling wheat to the Russians we might force up the price of wheat and create a shortage in this country.

As so frequently happens, the offended parties flew to Washington to protest this deal with their congressmen. Two men who owned bakeries in my district came to see me, so I took them to lunch in the Members Dining Room. I ordered a cheeseburger and french fries. Both bakers ordered the same. When lunch arrived, there were no buns on the plates. The bakers were indignant. "Where is the bread?" they asked.

"Yes," I added, "where's the bread?"

The waiter replied, "Why Mr. Zion, you never eat bread."

Butz Tells One Too Many

Earl Butz was a great agriculture secretary. He was also a great storyteller, but sometimes his stories were a touch insensitive.

I was on the board of directors of a small company with Earl and we couldn't get much done. Anything that was said reminded him of a story which he proceded to tell.

One fateful day in 1973 that is now legend, Earl was en route to a Republican convention in San Francisco. Entertainer Pat Boone was on the plane, and sitting next to him was Powell Moore, assistant to the President at the White House. John Dean, who was instrumental in exposing Watergate, came down the aisle and asked Boone if he could interview him when they landed. Dean was working for *Rolling Stone* magazine at the time. Powell Moore graciously got up and gave his seat to Dean so he could do his interviewing on the way to California.

About this time, Earl Butz came by and waved to Pat Boone. Pat is a good Republican and asked Earl how he was doing. They chatted a minute, and Boone asked Earl why it is that members of

Agriculture Secretary Earl Butz wishes me well after my defeat in 1974.

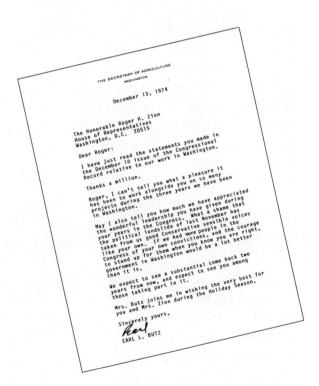

THE SECRETARY OF AGRICULTURE
WASHINGTON

December 13, 1974

The Honorable Roger H. Zion
House of Representatives
Washington, D.C. 20515

Dear Roger:

I have just read the statements you made in the December 10 issue of the Congressional Record relative to our work in Washington.

Thanks a million.

Roger, I can't tell you what a pleasure it has been to work alongside you on so many projects during the three years we have been in Washington.

May I also tell you how much we have appreciated the wonderful leadership you have given during your years in the Congress. What a shame that the political landslide of last November has taken from us good Conservative sensible voices like your own. If we had more people in the Congress of your own convictions, and the courage to stand up for them when you know you are right, government in Washington would be a lot better than it is.

We expect to see a substantial come back two years from now, and expect to see you among those taking part in it.

Mrs. Butz joins me in wishing the very best for you and Mrs. Zion during the Holiday Season.

Sincerely yours,

EARL L. BUTZ

69

the black race don't support Republicans more than they do. "After all, it was Abraham Lincoln that did the most for them," he observed.

At this point, Earl told one of his off-color stories that was derogatory to the black race.

John Dean reported it in *Rolling Stone,* it became infamous, and Butz resigned.

Boone wrote a note to Dean saying that he thought it was terribly indiscreet to publish a story that was told between friends, but the damage was done.

Butz was full of good advice, though. He told me that whenever I give a speech, I should remember the "three F's." A speech should always have some fun, some facts, and some filosophy.

Keith Plays to the Folks Back Home

Toward the end of each congressional year, members of Congress try to finish up all the work that got swept under the rug earlier in the session. This often results in late night sessions.

In 1972, we were debating a bill that proposed to establish large grain reserves in this country. It was well after midnight and there was considerably more heat than light being shed on the subject. As I recall the situation, some member expressed an aside that the American people ate too much grain already.

With this, Keith Sebelius, who represented one of the largest wheat producing areas in Kansas, took the microphone in the well of the House. After the speaker gaveled for order, Keith offered a suggestion to the membership that doubtless endeared him to the folks back home.

"Look, fellows," he said, "my people need a better market for their wheat. If you don't like bread or rolls, at least mess 'em up so they can't be served to someone else." He once offered an amendment to an agriculture bill that "Required cows to have twin calves—and double the meat production."

The Good Guys

Several of us got together every week or so and drove out to a place we called the chicken shack. It was a family-style restaurant that served big platters of chicken and large bowls of vegetables. Except for Dick Roudebush (who later headed the Veterans Administration), we all ate chicken and took "doggy bags" full when we left. "Roudy," who raised cattle back in Indiana, always ordered a steak.

We were all conservative members of Congress and called ourselves the "Good Guys." Once we decided to invite all the conservative members to a dinner and have President Nixon meet with us. That meeting was a success, so we repeated the process every month or so and invited a member of the Cabinet to join us. It was an "off the record" meeting.

The press was not invited and members were asked not to discuss anything that was said. Representative Phil Gramm, then a Democrat from Texas, met with us. He later became a Republican leader in the Senate.

Our program chairman lined up Alexander Haig, then chairman of the Joint Chiefs of Staff, for a talk in 1974, during the Vietnam War. Haig had been running back and forth to the battle zone. He held press conferences, reported to the President, met with military leaders in the U.S. and then flew back to Vietnam. He was a very busy man.

On the night he was to meet with us, he was about an hour late getting there. The guys were a bit restless but were anxious to get the lowdown on the war. Haig gave us a standard speech and paused for questions. Several members wanted to know some intimate details of what was going on, but Haig stuck to his basic text. Phil Crane and Ed Derwinski of Illinois and Herb Burke of Florida were insulted. "Hey, Al, we can get all that stuff in the newspapers. We want to really know what's going on, not just what you feed to the media," they told him.

Haig kept his cool, the members didn't, and the meeting ended with a feeling of hostility. I apologized for my associates' behavior when I left. It seemed to me that they were giving the general more problems than he needed, and I told him so. About a year later, Haig

71

Secretary of State Al Haig was a master of public relations.

became secretary of state and hired my former legislative assistant, Beldon Bell, to head his legislative team.

Haig was scheduled to give a talk at the Capitol Hill Club Headliner Breakfast. When I approached the club I saw Bell waiting for the general out in front. He was accompanied by the usual security people with the communication equipment, keeping in touch with Haig's car. I stopped to talk with Belden as the secretary of state's car drove up.

Haig got out and approached us. "You know my old boss, Roger Zion, don't you, Mr. Secretary?" Belden asked. Haig stuck out his hand and observed: "Yes, I certainly do—I hope this group is a little less hostile than the Good Guys."

FBI to the Rescue

President Nixon used to reward his faithful supporters and twist the arms of those who opposed him, on the presidential yacht, The Sequoia. A few members put out press releases saying that they refused these invitations because it was bribery and they wouldn't be a part of it. I told them I was already "had" and would go in their place.

One evening in early 1970, we were steaming down the Potomac when one of the congressmen decided to use the ship-to-shore phone to set up a late date. He apparently was a bit specific about what he wanted to do when he and his lady-friend got together.

The next morning he received a phone call from a man who had intercepted and recorded the conversation. The man felt he had something that he could sell at a considerable profit, and set up a meeting for that evening. He demanded cash for the tape. Our hero was concerned. He didn't want to part with considerable cash and didn't want to encourage more future bribe demands.

He decided to call Attorney General John Mitchell for advice. Mitchell sent some FBI agents to meet with the Congressman an hour before the scheduled meeting. They equipped him with a hidden recorder and sent him on his way. He was told to engage the man in enough conversation to show that he was asking for a bribe.

Though this wasn't his cup of tea, the congressman met his adversary at the edge of a wooded park as he had agreed. The man was as nervous as the victim. After a bit of uneasy sparring, the two got down to business. The congressman asked the crook to agree not to make any additional copies of the tape and got him to agree that the money he was about to receive was all that he would ever request.

At this point the bushes exploded with F.B.I. men. They cited some federal statutes about bribery, shook the guy up pretty well, told him they had recorded his bribe attempt and, in general, scared the living daylights out of him. The poor guy apologized profusely, swore he wouldn't do it again, and left with his tail between his legs.

I'm sure our friend, the Congressman, made no more calls of an explicit nature. And if he did, they weren't made on a ship-to-shore phone.

Agnew's "John"

Once I was taking a small group of people on a tour of the Capitol. Among my tourists was my teenage son, Randy. A highlight of the tour was a visit to Vice President Spiro Agnew's office. Randy was interested in all the historic objects around the office. A beautiful chandelier had once been in the White House during Teddy Roosevelt's presidency. Since there wasn't air conditioning in those days, the windows were open and the breeze caused the crystals on the chandelier to tinkle. The noise bothered the President, so he directed: "Take that thing over to the Vice President's office. Maybe it will keep him awake." It's been there ever since.

There is also a gold-framed mirror hanging near the ceiling where no one can see in it. According to the folklore, Dolly Madison bought the mirror in France. Her husband was upset about it for some reason so he hung it where it couldn't be used.

Randy noticed the name "Mike Mansfield" clearly imprinted in Agnew's desktop. Apparently the majority leader of the Senate at that time had signed something on the V.P.'s desk and the name had gone through the paper to the surface of the desk.

Vice President Spiro Agnew—the first big smudge on the Nixon administration.

The hotline phone directly to the White House was interesting, as was the clock that had been ticking for years but mysteriously stopped at about the time the clockmaker died.

I noticed that Randy opened a small door in one wall but didn't pay much attention to it at the time. Years later, I visited Randy and his wife at their apartment in Nashville. In a small powder room was a picture frame holding a scrap of toilet paper. Under the frame was a note: "taken from Agnew's john," and the date of his visit.

Dennis the Menace

Dave Dennis was the most active legislator in the Indiana delegation. He studied every piece of legislation and usually had some comments to make on every bill that came up.

While he was a great legislator, he wasn't much of politician. I remember once he was asked to send a flag that had been flown over the Capitol to an American Legion post. "I'm here to legislate," he told his staff, "not to fly flags."

While most of us took special efforts to visit with constituents and have our pictures taken with them on Capitol steps, Dave was too busy with his legislative activities. He even failed to make a fundraising dinner in his own district. The emcee read a telegram to the assembled guests from the Congressman. It should have read, "I regret that congressional duties preclude my attending your banquet." Unfortunately the word duties was misspelled as "cuties."

Wolf Man Don

Don Young, Alaska's only Congressman, is a fisherman, trapper, hunter, ex-riverboat pilot, and schoolteacher. Mostly, he's an enthusiastic representative of his constituents. One day he got so involved in a debate on the House floor that he hyperventilated and broke out in a rash. The Capitol physician prescribed a game of paddleball until he calmed down.

When Big Don gets into a debate, there is absolutely no ques-

Henry Kissinger is one of the greatest authorities on foreign affairs we have ever had.

The question furthest from my mind at this encounter with Attorney General John Mitchell: How much did he know about Watergate?

tion where he is coming from. One day, there was a bill on the floor that would outlaw animal traps. The animal lovers claimed that traps were cruel. Young explained that traps weren't painful; they just held the animal until the hunter came and mercifully harvested the game.

To prove his point he stuck his hand in a trap. It snapped and clamped down. "See," explained Don, "It doesn't hurt; it just holds." He walked into the cloakroom, broke out in a sweat and almost fainted from the pain.

Later, an advocate of saving the timber wolf brought one of the endangered animals to the Interior Committee hearing room. He pointed out that these beasts were getting a bad rap. "They aren't dangerous to humans and can be domesticated," he explained.

Being a great naturalist, Young went over to pat the wolf. It bit him. Ever since then, Big Don's name has been Wolf Man.

Henry's Women

During the Nixon Administration I served on a White House energy task force that met occasionally in the President's board room. He had a long oval table where he met with his cabinet and conducted other gatherings of significance. At one meeting I sat next to Vice President Agnew and across from Secretary of State Henry Kissinger. John Ehrlichman was the chairman of the meeting and called on various participants to discuss areas within their particular fields of expertise.

It was before Henry Kissinger's much-publicized wedding to Nancy. At that time, he was very much the man-about-town. In recognizing the Secretary of State, John Ehrlichman said, "Many people wonder why Henry isn't married. He responds that he wants to preserve his options. From what I've seen of his girlfriends, they are remarkably well preserved."

D.C. Dangers

Marjorie Holt was a very capable Congresswoman from Maryland. She tells an improbable tale of her first few weeks in office. After being elected from an area that included Annapolis, Maryland, the site of the Naval Academy and one of the safer areas on the East Coast, she was afraid to move to the District of Columbia because of the frightening crime statistics. Instead, she commuted the hour-long drive to the Capitol twice a day.

One morning she overheard a tradesman talking to her staff in the outer office. He was telling them of his many years in Washington and his belief that the District was certainly a safe place to live. He could see no reason why members of Congress and their staffs shouldn't move in and live a safe and happy life in our nation's capital. Marjorie was anxious to be reassured, so she joined the conversation. In the course of the discussion, she asked him what line of work he was in. He quipped, "I'm a tailgunner on a laundry truck."

Verbosity Unappreciated

Members of Congress are frequently and justifiably accused of being unnecessarily verbose. When I was in Congress, I tried to get home at least every weekend to see how the family was getting along, check on constituent problems. etc. One weekend, however, was spent in a much publicized junket to Beirut, Lebanon, attending an international road-building seminar. While I was gone my young son, Randy, was especially inquisitive. "Where is Daddy? Why isn't he home? What's he doing in Lebanon?"

My wife tried patiently to explain my absence and the importance of the trip, but finally in desperation replied to an especially tough question, "Why not ask your dad when he gets home?"

Randy didn't bat an eye and said, "I won't ask Daddy because I don't want to know that much about it!"

Corporal Price Promoted

New committee chairmen are entitled to have their portraits hung in the committee hearing room. Mel Price of Illinois, having replaced Ed Herbert as chairman of the Armed Services Committee, was having his portrait hung in the main committee hearing room in 1975.

Accordingly, his friends and associates gathered for a very nice reception suitable for a man of his prominence. Bob Wilson of California, ranking Republican on the committee, was the emcee. Speaker "Tip" O'Neill and other dignitaries spoke, but the best talk was delivered by the modest, unassuming recipient of the honor, the Honorable Mel Price, himself.

He recalled that he was a corporal in the Army at Fort Lee, Virginia, when his brother called him from home to tell him he had been elected to Congress. It is rather informally presumed by socialites who seat dinner guests according to protocol that a member of Congress ranks at about the level of a three-star general. It was thus quite a promotion for Corporal Price.

Word of his election spread throughout the camp and created quite a ripple. The colonel immediately started introducing him to other officers. The commanding general sent his staff car to pick up Mel for an audience in the general's office.

When Corporal Price started to salute, the General extended his hand and barked an order to his aide: "From now on, when a man in my command is elected to Congress, he automatically is promoted one step up. Congratulations, Sergeant Price!"

Ghost Congressman

A second portrait was hung the same day in the Minority Leader's conference room in the Capitol. It was in honor of Les Arends of Illinois, who had served in the House of Representatives for forty years and under seven Presidents. Les had been Minority Whip for many of those years and was loved on both sides of the aisle.

He graciously accepted the portrait that we had commissioned for him and told of his many friends and fond memories. One of his greatest friends was Mendel Rivers of South Carolina. Both of them stood tall and straight, and both had long, flowing, white hair. If any two congressmen looked the perfect picture of senior statesmen, they were Mendel and Les.

One evening they were standing together behind the rail on the House Floor while the Clerk called the role. Although the Clerks very seldom err, there is a first time for everything. Partly from habit, he called the name of Congressman Andresen of Minnesota, who had died six months earlier.

"Les," said Mendel, "if he answers the roll, let's get the hell out of here!"

Fleeting Fame

A year after President Ford was deposed, Representative Paul Simon of Illinois sent a letter to "Honorable Gerald R. Ford, c/o P.O. Box, Washington, D.C." It was returned to him marked "Return to Sender."

Fame and fortune — well fame at least — is indeed fleeting!

Lessons From the House Sage

Doubtless the epitome of wit and wisdom in the House was the late Tennyson Guyer, Congressman from Ohio. Tenny was a circus clown, public relations director, ordained minister, social worker, and state senator prior to his election to the U.S. Congress. He probably made more speeches than any other member of Congress, having to his credit at least 1,000 commencement addresses and speeches in twenty-four foreign countries. It was impossible to spend ten minutes with him without being amused and spiritually uplifted.

During one breakfast meeting with him, he gave me the following things to think about: Concerning a colleague of ours not noted for his effectiveness in Congress, "He has been riding the crest of a slump...He has a great future behind him...One thing about being as mediocre as he is, he never has a bad day...Can really cheer up a room by walking out of it."

Tenny always felt a need to perform community service and said that such service is the rent we pay to God for the privilege of enjoying his great earth.

He told me that good judgment comes from experience and that good experience comes from bad judgment.

On responsibility, he advised that if we kicked the person responsible for most of our individual problems, we couldn't sit down for a week.

Wrong Wright

Norm Dicks was elected to Congress from Washington State in 1980, but before that, he was an aide to the famous Senator Warren Magnuson. One of "Maggy's" big constituents was the Boeing Aircraft company. Boeing was anxious to build theS.S.T. (Super Sonic Transport plane) and Maggy wanted to help all he could. One of the problems was that many environmentalists claimed that the plane would fly into the stratosphere and disrupt the ozone balance. Other opponents thought that the federal cost was too high.

A bill to fund the S.S.T. was before the House Ways and Means Committee, so Senator Magnuson called Chairman Wilbur Mills to lobby in favor of it. "Orville," he said. "We've been friends for a long time. I really need this project for my state. Hundreds of jobs depend on it. Please, Orville, do what you can to get this project approved, will you?

When he hung up he turned to then-aide Dicks and asked, "How did I do?" Norm looked at him and responded: "You did fine, but you've got the wrong Wright brother. The chairman's name is Wilbur, not Orville."

Well, Maggy was pretty upset. The next time he saw Mills, he apologized profusely. "I'm sorry I called you Orville. I knew you were Wilbur."

"I'm sorry, too," Wilbur replied. "Actually my father wanted to name me Orville, but my mother objected. Frankly, I'd rather be named Orville than Wilbur."

From that day on, whenever Senator Magnuson talked to Congressman Mills, he called him Orville.

Congressmen are Crooks

Leon Panetta of California was campaigning in front of a grocery store when a lady refused to take the literature he was handing out. After pursuing her a short distance, it was apparent she was not interested. In fact, she told him, "I don't know if you are a Republican or Democrat — whether you are seeking office or already hold one — you're all a bunch of crooks!"

"Panetta is not a crook," responded the candidate defensively.

"Panetta? What kind of name is Panetta?" the lady asked.

"Italian," Leon responded.

"Ah, ha!" she cried. "Just what I thought — you're all a bunch of crooks!"

Everyone Loves a Candidate

This reminded me of a time back in 1964 when I was campaigning for the House with Russell Bontrager who was running for the Senate. We found a little old lady who refused our literature. What made it especially disappointing was that the TV cameras were recording our efforts at the time. When Russ pursued her and finally got her to take the literature, she threw it on the ground and stomped on it. While the cameras turned, and without changing expression, Russ said to our helpers, "Let's put her down as doubtful."

Everyone's a Voter

Bill Nichols of Alabama was a fighter for his district. He agreed with most members that we should curtail foreign aid, which is described as any money spent outside one's own Congressional district. But he favors additional spending for his constituents.

During the debate on a waterflood authorization bill, Congressman Nichols complained that a recent flood had washed away the skeletons of eight Indians from an old cemetery. One of Bill's cohorts was heard to whisper, "That's terrible, Bill has been voting those Indians for years."

Useful Money

H.R. Gross of Iowa was the most conscientious member in the House. He never missed a debate and seldom stayed out of important ones. Back in the mid-sixties the House was discussing the issuance of new "sandwich" coins which had less inherent value than those made with silver.

H.R. strode down to the well of the House, swinging a long string to which he had tied a handful of nuts and bolts. "As long as we are going to trade wampum," he advised, "why don't we use beads or shells like the Indians used. Or I have a better idea; let's use nuts and bolts. The way our money is being devaluated, it won't be worth much anyway. If we make it out of nuts and bolts, we could at least use it to repair the washing machine."

All in Your Point of View

One day I pointed out Gross to a constituent as we stood on the balcony overlooking the House floor. A Democratic member was doing the same in the row behind me. I explained to my guest that Gross was one of the most effective and productive members of the House.

Meanwhile, the member behind me was also pointing to Gross

and telling his constituent that Gross was "the biggest obstructionist in the House."

Which Way Does the Wind Blow?

Tom Milligan, former Republican state chairman from Indiana, likes to show the way politicians avoid taking a stand on an issue. As an example, he quotes Senator Jim Watson, who served during the difficult Prohibition era. When asked how he stood on prohibition, he always took a long pause, looked thoughtful, and responded, "Some of my friends drink and some of them don't drink. Some favor the prohibition of drinking and some oppose it. As for my position, I'm for my friends."

So Long, Pal

Saudi Arabia began prohibiting the use of alcohol for its citizens in 1953. Our ambassador at the time was known for his love of spirituous ferment, and complained to Prince Faisal, "I'm sure something can be done about this, can't it?" he asked.

"Of course, Excellency," the prince responded, "and we shall miss you."

Hindsight is Best

President Ford spoke to a meeting of former congressmen at a White House reception in the spring of 1975. We had all enjoyed the opportunity of giving him our best advice over the usual hors d'oeuvres and cocktails in the Lincoln dining room. During a lull in the conversational buzzing, he spoke a few words.

"It's a great treat to be here at the fifth annual gathering of the Former Members of Congress. This is the one organization whose members really have it made. You can sleep late each morning, get up when you feel like it, listen to the birds sing, linger over your coffee, spend two hours reading the paper, then — this is the best part — you can turn to your wife and complain about the mess they're making in Washington."

Susan's Gift

Soon after Gerald Ford succeeded Nixon in the White House, Ford's daughter, Susan, decided to give her father a dog for Christmas. After some discussion, she decided on a Golden Retriever. She called a kennel that was well recommended and asked if she could buy a pup. The kennel owner wanted to be sure the dog had a good home and wondered who the new owner would be. Susan didn't want the secret to leak out and didn't want to tell him it was for the President, but she did relieve his mind somewhat. She told him that the owner was a friendly, middle-aged man who lived in a large, white house with a big yard and a fence around it. She had a little trouble answering whether the new owner had a steady job and whether he rented or owned his home, but she must have gotten around it somehow because the President was the happy owner of a loving retriever named Liberty.

Joining the Heathen

Years ago, Congressman Walter Judd of Minnesota started a prayer breakfast club. It is limited to members and past members of Congress and it still meets every Thursday morning in the Capitol building.

The Members take turns being discussion leaders. It is a most refreshing experience, plus being a source of some interesting stories.

A freshman member was telling of the effect his election had on his family. His wife and three small children were most excited about their move to Washington, but also a bit concerned about how the move would affect their school, Sunday school, etc.

One night they discovered just how profound that effect would be. They overheard their six-year-old son saying his prayers the night before they were going to leave. At the end of the prayer, the young tyke concluded, "Well, goodbye, God. We're moving to Washington."

William Simon Calls Back

When I first met Bill Simon, he was secretary of energy and I was chairman of a task force on energy and resources. Bill later became a very good treasury secretary. He always came to our task force meetings if he could. If his schedule didn't permit, we tried to change the date to accommodate him. He was a very interested and knowledgeable participant.

One day in 1972 I called his office and asked for him. His secretary said he was tied up and asked me for my schedule so he could call me back. I guess I was a tad flippant; I told her everything I planned to do for the next week, including my weekend.

On the next Sunday morning, I was just going to tee-off on the first hole of the Evansville Country Club when the public address system called me. It was Simon. He was in his office working and had just gotten around to me. He always called back.

A few years later I got a call from Earl Butz, ex-secretary of agriculture. He wanted me to help him form a "Simon for President" committee. I told him I thought that Bill Simon was one of the smartest, most capable men I had ever known, but that he had been so honest and called it like it was to the extent that he had killed every sacred cow in Washington. "He'd be a terrific President," I told Earl, "but we couldn't get him elected."

At least two years after that, Simon was scheduled to be the guest speaker at a fundraiser for the Capitol Hill Club. He had written a book and a friend of mine had a copy that he wanted autographed. I invited him to the breakfast and took him up to meet ex-Secretary Simon.

"Hi, Roger," Bill smiled, "you are certainly right. I have killed every sacred cow in Washington and couldn't get elected."

When Simon retired from Treasury in 1976, I wrote him a letter thanking him for his valuable service to our country.

Not Me

Bob Orr was a good friend, neighbor, tennis partner, precinct committeeman, county chairman, state senator, lieutenant governor, and governor. He also became a very fine ambassador to Singapore.

Among his many favorable traits is a good sense of humor. One day in 1973, Bob and I were riding in an antique Packard convertible down Evansville's Main Street. It was Labor Day and we were looking for exposure. I was hoping to be reelected to Congress and Bob was running for the State Senate.

I was always a bit embarrassed to be so obviously seeking publicity, so I pretended to see people I knew in the street-side crowd and waved to them. "Hi, George," or "Hi, Milly," I would shout. Of course, people thought I really knew someone and it gave me a "homey" look. As Dick Schulze, Congressman from Pennsylvania, puts it: "The most important quality in politics is sincerity, and once you learn to fake that, you've got it made."

As we rounded a corner, some man ran up to the car and started booing. He was obviously irate. Veins stood out on his neck. I've never seen such a picture of outright hatred.

Bob and I looked at each other and each said at the same time, "That guy doesn't like you."

Chapter Four

Early in 1969, President Chung Hee Park of the Republic of Korea asked me to be co-chairman of a program to broadcast across the bamboo curtain to the people of Southeast Asia. Since former First Lady Mamie Eisenhower had agreed to be the other chairperson, how could I refuse?

The South Korean government leased their broadcast facilities to Radio of Free Asia so that they could put pressure on Hanoi to abide by the provisions of the Geneva convention. I made speeches about the cruel and inhumane treatment of our prisoners, and the speeches were translated into various languages and then sent over the airwaves from Korea.

President Chung Hee Park wrote to me: "In the struggle against communism, no weapon is more effective than the truth. Radio of Free Asia is serving as a Bridge of Truth reaching out to millions of oppressed people behind the bamboo curtain. Korea is very happy to provide the base for this operation. No other nation on this Earth is more committed to this sacred fight than Korea. Communist neighbors surrounding us are ever increasing their hostilities to our free Korea and other free nations in Asia. Yet Korea is one nation determined to live up to the utterance of your famous countryman Patrick Henry's 'Give us liberty or give us death.' You have my genuine gratitude and my high esteem as a champion for freedom."

Pat Linder, Super Hero

In mid-1970 a woman named Pat Linder came into my office and asked if we wanted a HERO. She explained that HERO stood for Help Elect Republican Office Holders. These people had time to spare and wanted to volunteer their services in Republican offices.

Bob Junk, my administrative assistant, welcomed her and gave her a desk in the front of the office, where she sorted mail, answered correspondence and acted as a receptionist.

We had a deaf intern at the time, and Pat learned sign language so she could communicate with him.

Pat's husband was Admiral Linder, who was stationed at the Pentagon. He had been captain of an aircraft carrier from which flyers flew over Vietnam. Some of them hadn't returned, and Pat kept up a letter exchange with their families. She was active with the prisoners of war and missing in action groups around the world.

One day in July of 1970, she asked me to sponsor a "National Week of Concern for Prisoners of War/Missing in Action." The Joint House/Senate Resolution, signed by President Richard Nixon, urged Americans to write to the delegate general of North Vietnam in Paris demanding that he conform to the provisions of the Geneva conventions, as it applied to POW/MIA's.

At the same time, I wrote a letter to Pham Van Dong, the premier of the Democratic Republic of Vietnam, expressing the outrage of the members of the U.S. House of Representatives for the failure of the North Vietnamese and Viet Cong to provide access to the Red Cross and to permit exchange of mail, provide medical care, etc. The letter was signed by every member of the House but two. "Doc" Hall of Missouri and H.R. Gross of Iowa (very conservative members) refused to sign the letter because it began "Your Excellency." If it had started, "You S.O.B.," they would have signed it. I sent the letter to the North Vietnam headquarters in Paris and asked for an appointment to see them.

During the next two weeks I traveled to Europe and spoke to the parliaments of several nations, urging them to put pressure on North Vietnam to abide by the Geneva Convention. All of these procedures were quarterbacked by Pat Linder.

While I was trying to put pressure on the Vietnamese, Jane Fonda and Ramsey Clark were in Southeast Asia trying to get our fighting men to quit. Among other expressions, Fonda said that we should get on our knees and pray for a communist victory.

On the House floor, Father Bob Drinan, a member from Massachusetts, was a spokesman for her and her point of view. I once asked him, in a debate on funding for the House Committee on Internal Security, if we would be permitted to pray if we had a communist victory in this country.

The committee was holding hearings on subversive organizations. I tried to subpoena both Fonda and Clark and charge them with treason. The majority members of the committee didn't go along but they did ask Clark to come before us.

A prominent news magazine featured a picture of an unexploded bomb on the surface of the ground near a North Vietnamese hospital. In the picture was Ramsey Clark, claiming that the U.S. Air Force was bombing civilian hospitals and should be condemned. He wanted military leaders to be charged with war crimes.

In the week before Clark appeared before the committee, we heard testimony from Air Force officers who said that a bomb dropped from their planes couldn't possibly stay on the surface, but would dig a crater and be far below the surface of the ground. They denied bombing hospitals.

When I asked how the bomb could be found so near a hospital, the officer said it was obviously dragged there for propaganda purposes. I quoted them for Clark and asked for his comment. He didn't have one.

We showed letters from subversive organizations that cited Clark's work on their behalf and asked him if he was a member of these communist-front groups. He refused to explain his association with them.

Since he had two cohorts on the committee (Drinan and Claude Pepper) and since we had no direct evidence of his membership in these anti-American groups, we let him go.

Confrontation in Paris

I waited for two or three weeks for Pham Van Dong to respond to my letter. When it was apparent that I wasn't going to hear from him, Pat Linder suggested that I go to Paris and meet with Mai Van Bo, the delegate general of the Vietnamese Peace Mission.

There were many wives of missing flyers in Paris at the time, and they had repeatedly been turned away from the Vietnam compound. Pat thought that if I held press conferences featuring these women, I might finally break Mai Van Bo down and he would see me.

Discussing the critical prisoner-of-war situation with me are (l-r) Colonel Frank Borman, the president's special consultant on prisoners of war; Navy Lieutenant David Matheny; and Major James N. Rowe. Matheny and Rowe had been POWs.

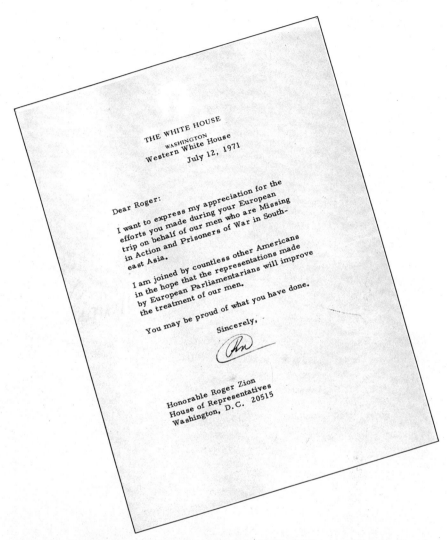

THE WHITE HOUSE
WASHINGTON
Western White House
July 12, 1971

Dear Roger:

I want to express my appreciation for the efforts you made during your European trip on behalf of our men who are Missing in Action and Prisoners of War in Southeast Asia.

I am joined by countless other Americans in the hope that the representations made by European Parliamentarians will improve the treatment of our men.

You may be proud of what you have done.

Sincerely,

Rn

Honorable Roger Zion
House of Representatives
Washington, D.C. 20515

Appearing on this stationery, "Rn" is none other than Richard Nixon, writing to tell me he appreciated my efforts on behalf of prisoners of war and servicemen missing in action.

I headed for Paris in late 1971 with that in mind. As soon as the State Department learned that I was going, they alerted a Southeast Asia authority and asked him to meet me at the American Embassy in Paris. Fred Flott was then assistant to Ambassador Henry Cabot Lodge in Saigon. He became a valuable partner in the project. We checked into a hotel near the American Embassy and met with Ambassador Arthur Watson. He assigned Philip Habib to work with us. Habib was senior advisor to the U.S. Peace Mission on Vietnam in Paris. He later was assistant Secretary of State and a special representative for Middle East peace talks.

Habib told us that the Vietnamese refused to respond to any overtures from the U.S. government. There had been many diplomatic attempts to see them but they all failed.

"Maybe it's time for hard ball," he told me. "You have to work independently from the embassy. We haven't done well. You are completely on your own."

Flott and I contacted a group of POW wives and called a press conference. The wives made pathetic references to the cruelty of the Vietnamese and made references to the Geneva Convention. We made frequent use of the expression "cruel and inhumane treatment."

After three days of press conferences with different POW/MIA families, I received a phone call from Mai Van Bo's office.

"Deputy Zion," the caller said. "General Van Bo will see you for fifteen minutes tomorrow morning at 10:00."

This was the breakthrough we wanted. I rushed over to the embassy to tell Flott and Habib of the meeting. At first they offered to drive me in an embassy car but changed their minds. "You are on your own. We'll only hurt your chances," they told me. "Take a cab."

The next morning, I left early for the Vietnam compound. We had dumped tons of mail on their doorstep as a result of our letter-writing campaign during the national week of concern for POWs/MIAs, so they knew we had a big following. My work with the European Parliaments had resulted in giving them a black eye in the court of world opinion and there was some evidence that they were becoming self-conscious about their image.

The cab got me there about a half-hour early so I dropped into a restaurant and sipped a glass of orange juice.

At the appointed time I knocked on the door of the Vietnam compound. I was admitted and escorted to a small room with three chairs. I was wearing contact lenses during the meeting which lasted almost an hour. In the middle of the interview something lodged in my eye, behind the lens. It felt like a chunk of glass. I was afraid that if I took it out and popped it in my mouth to clean it off, General Van Bo would think I was taking a cyanide capsule, or something similar, so I stood the pain. I wondered if the tears streaming down my face added to my presentation or showed signs of weakness.

At the close of the discussion, Van Bo handed me a can containing a movie film. He said it was a film taped at a Christmas party for POWs and showed that the captors were very humane indeed.

I took the film, went out into the street and hailed a cab. Suddenly I felt exhausted. All the efforts that led up to the confrontation, all the pressure I felt from the hopes of the POW/MIA families, and the meeting itself, had taken their toll.

I rode up to my hotel and checked the door to my room. There was hair glued across the space between the door and the door jamb. I had been told to expect that. It was a method for someone to check my coming and going. I was also told that my phone was probably tapped. Every time I came to my room, I found the hair in place.

I still have no idea who was checking on me. Was it the French? the Vietnamese? Our CIA?

In any event, I went into the room, threw the film on the bed and walked to the embassy.

Quite a crowd had assembled. The ambassador, Habib, Flott, many staff members and twenty or so family members of POW/ MIAs were anxiously awaiting my report.

I was debriefed by staff people who knew what they were doing. What did Van Bo look like? Did he speak English? What did the interpreter look like? Did I see anyone else? etc., etc.

During the debriefing I mentioned the film. "What film?!!" I was asked. "Where is it?" "It's on the bed in my hotel room," I told them. I'd never seen such excitement.

Several staff people grabbed my hotel key and ran down the street to get the film.

When they got back, a projector had been set up and everyone was breathlessly waiting to see who could be identified at the so-called "Christmas Party."

The pictures were dark and of poor quality. Every now and then, as the movie progressed, someone would squeal, "It's him! It's John! He looks terrible, but he's alive!"

You can't imagine the effect of this movie on the people who were watching. The full range of emotions was evident, from total exhuberation to total despair. It was an extremely emotional experience. The film was shown several times, and each time some ghostly figure as tentatively identified.

After the showing, the Embassy staff served punch and cookies. Someone suggested that we should celebrate this breakthrough by taking me out to dinner. We decided to meet at eight o'clock.

I went back to my hotel, noticed a new hair had been placed on my door, and tried to take a nap. I'm not very good at daytime napping, so I went for a long walk. At eight, I joined Fred Flott, two embassy assistants and three women who had identified their husbands. Dinner was completely occupied by discussion of the film. It was apparent that there was considerable doubt about the positive identification of the POWs.

They were all thinner, the pictures were dark, and it was possible that someone desperately wanting to see a loved one could do some wishful thinking.

Dining in Paris is a long and tiresome experience and I didn't get back to the hotel until late. When I got to my room the phone was ringing. It was a reporter whom I knew from CBS news, calling from Washington. The word was out that I had a film showing a group of POWs. He wanted to know when I was going to arrive in D.C. and if I would let him borrow the film so he could put it on the evening news. I said, "O.K.," and he said he would meet me at the airport.

The next morning, Fred Flott and I were flying back to Washington. Fred had talked to the state department and to the defense department. A representative of Mel Laird, secretary of defense, was to meet us at the airport. They were going to take the film to the Pentagon, make 8x10 copies of each frame, and send them to military bases all around the world. It was hoped that they could identify some MIAs as POWs.

Whoops! I told Fred that I had already promised the film to my friend from CBS.

"What can I do now?" I asked.

"Nothing," Flott replied. "I hereby confiscate the film in the name of the state department. You must turn it over."

I wasn't sure of his right to take my film, but I gave it to him, anyway. When we got to D.C., the reporter was waiting for me. I explained, rather lamely, that the film had been confiscated and that I didn't have it.

He was furious! "I've scheduled the film for showing tonight," he told me. "I've told my boss that I had a scoop. You've got to give it to me."

"Sorry," I told him. "The national priority seems to preclude a news release until families have a chance to identify their members." He wasn't at all satisfied but I didn't know what else to do.

Early the next morning I called William Paley, chairman of CBS, to apologize. When I explained the whole scenario, he understood perfectly. "You did exactly what you should," he told me. "The national interest certainly is more important than our news scoop." I felt a lot better.

Since that time I have met with several POW groups and individuals. They report that their treatment was somewhat improved as a result of the mass of adverse publicity that the North Vietnamese received from the international community.

In the fall of 1991, I attended a regular prayer breakfast in the Capitol. The speaker was Congressman Douglas "Pete" Peterson of Florida, who told of his terrible experience as a POW captive of the Vietnamese. I loaned him my film and the documents that went with it.

He showed the film to his staff people. In the middle of the film he shouted, "That's me standing next to Alvarez." He recognized himself and several other former POWs. This is what he had to say about the experience:

Christmas 1969 was a very special time for me. For the first time, formal religious services were held at the Zoo for both Catholic and Prot-

estant groups. However, not all POWs were allowed to attend the services. For whatever reason, I was selected along with approximately thirty others to attend Catholic mass. We were not asked if we wanted to go; we were simply told to go. We were all taken separately to the building we called the Auditorium where for the first time at the Zoo we actually mingled with other prisoners. Although one can see in the film that everyone was very reluctant to attempt to strike up a conversation with anyone else and most of us were even careful not to look around very much. This was a learned behavior after having been bashed around a lot for attempting to see other prisoners during our movements around the camp and in our activities there.

The place was well decorated and lighted to accommodate TV cameras. The cameras were a turnoff to most of us as we were aware that the V had previously used events like this to produce films demonstrating how well we were being treated. This event was clearly intended to do the same thing, but on the positive side turned out to be very beneficial for a number of families who still did not have conclusive evidence that we were alive.

Al Alvarez and I walked into the room together for Mass. I had never had any previous contact with any of the men with me that day. The film that was subsequently played back in the U.S. and the one that I have just recently reviewed again in Washington has only a brief shot of me and Alvarez. Nevertheless, that brief shot was enough for my wife to identify me from the film when she was able to see it in the fall of 1971.

Carlotta, my wife, was living in Fort Walton Beach, Florida, while I was gone. She was called one night after the evening national news by her family in Mariana, Florida, saying they thought they had seen me on film strip on the evening news. A friend who was the news director at a Dothan, Alabama, T.V. station offered to run the film for Carlotta at the station.

She went to Dothan and, after several runs, adamantly insisted that she had identified me in the film. Unfortunately, she was told later by Air Force authorities that about ten other families had identified me as their husband, brother or father.

The film taken at the Christmas party in 1969 was a very important factor in my family's ability to sustain themselves during the last three years of my captivity. It was not for another several months after the emergence of the film that Carlotta was officially notified that I was a confirmed POW.

Ambassador Mamie

In the early 1970s, in the midst of the war, some Capitol Hill staffers decided to do something for the men and women who were patients in the two military hospitals in Washington. Mary Ellen Terseau, who worked for Congressman John Buchanan, started a program which she called operation NOEL (No One Ever Lonely). She called on a lot of other staffers and members and took up a pretty good collection of money to pay for the project.

She and her committee sent invitations to both Bethesda Naval Hospital and Walter Reed Army Hospital. The committee asked me and Mamie Eisenhower to host the affair. On the appointed date, the Longworth House cafeteria was decorated like a high school prom. A small orchestra was engaged and a big buffet was spread out along one wall.

Busloads of sick and wounded service people streamed in. Most of the admirals and generals who were in town showed up.

The hit of the show, though, was Mamie. Everyone wanted to meet her and shake her hand.

I remember taking her around so that she could meet everyone personally. Once we got caught in a small snag of people between tables. A young staffer was in front of Mamie, but didn't see her trying to get through. Without hesitation, Mamie snapped her in the fanny with an experienced flip of the hand. The girl jumped a foot, turned with fire in her eyes, saw Mamie, smiled and let her slip by.

I remember that the patients had a good time and stayed until late in the evening. I especially remember a young man who had lost a leg. He tossed aside his crutches and really "cut a rug" with one of the hostesses on the dance floor.

It was a very refreshing and satisfying affair, but I'm sure none of the poison pen newspeople covered it. They are so busy looking for something to criticize that they overlook the many great things that come out of Capitol Hill.

Outshining even the generals in attendance, Mamie Eisenhower was truly the star of our big show of support for military patients in Washington during the Vietnam War. That's Alaskan Congressman Howard Pollack on the right.

Wives of prisoners of war show us "Tiger Cages" similar to those their husbands were detained in. As the women intended, it gave us a good idea of what conditions must have been like for POWs.

One of my good friends is Kathy Wei, world champion bridge player.

Chapter Five

When Vice President Spiro Agnew was being charged with all kinds of improprieties, Barry Goldwater came to his rescue. Barry called a bunch of us together in his conference room and told us we should "get out there and tell the truth" about our faithful vice president.

"He is the victim of the left-wing press," we were told. "He's as honest as the day is long," etc. Barry told us that left-wing agitators were following Agnew around the country trying to get something on him. He related that his wife, Peggy, had sent Agnew a painting that he had admired. Later, the artist was asked who paid for it, the questioners no doubt hoping that someone with an interest in influencing the government had done so. Actually, Peggy had paid for it and the artist told them so.

Barry said that snoopers were checking country clubs where Agnew played golf, trying to see who had picked up the tab. We were convinced that Agnew was indeed the innocent victim of a conspiracy.

Bill Dickinson of Alabama found a big poster with the picture of a cat hanging by its paws from a broom stick. He wrote, "Hang in there Spiro" on it, and took it to the cloakroom for his friends to sign. Many of us did.

I called my press secretary, Angela, and asked her to meet me at the House recording studio, where we produced "simulcasts" for the media. Angela would ask me questions and I would respond; the T.V. tape would go to the TV stations, a sound tape would go to the radio, and Angela would type up the script and send it to the print media. On this particular day, I was prepared to do a big pro-Agnew production.

An hour or so later, I was on the House Floor when the news buzzed around that Agnew had pleaded *Nolo Contendere* (I don't claim I did and I don't claim I didn't).

This meant that he didn't admit guilt but that he was subject to conviction.

Yipes!! I called Angela right away. "Have you sent out the Agnew stuff yet?" I asked.

"No, but I'm working as fast as I possibly can," she answered, a bit irritated.

"You know that place down in the studio where you can demagnetize the tapes?" I asked.

"Of course," she responded.

"O.K.—see that you use it," I told her. Whew!! I asked Dickinson what happened to the "Hang in there" poster. It seems that a reporter from a prominent news magazine had taken a picture of it. When the next issue hit the street, the picture was featured in a story about Agnew. Some of the signatures were indistinct. Mine was.

Goldwater Makes a Funny

The story goes that when Barry was running for President he was invited to play a round of golf at the exclusive Westchester Country Club.

An awkward situation arose when he was told that Jews were not permitted to participate in this club's activities.

"Hey, I'm only half Jewish," Goldwater told them. "How about me playing just nine holes."

Goldwater told me that one time he was on a plane to Washington from Phoenix. Sitting across the aisle was a young honeymooning couple that had not flown before.

Apparently they had filled up on a drug that was supposed to prevent air sickness. It also made them drowsy. The man fell asleep. The poor girl tried to hold back, but finally "tossed her cookies" all over him and her, too. She cleaned herself up as best she could. When he woke up and looked at his shirt front, he was amazed. "Feeling better?" she asked him.

Ruck Learns About Clean Air

Bill Ruckelshaus was a good attorney general and twice was head of the Environmental Protection Agency. His first political experience was as a state senator in Indiana. It was from that base that he ran for the national Senate seat and lost to incumbent Senator Vance Hartke.

Every two years I used to rent a helicopter and, starting at dawn at the east end of my district, dropped in to every town in Southern Indiana. We had press conferences lined up a every stop.

If there was a gubernatorial or senate race, I always invited the top state G.O.P. candidate to go with me. It gave him good exposure and allowed me to say a lot of good things about him.

Well, there was always some county chairman who didn't get the word or wanted it done his way. Seth Dembo was a case in point.

It was 1967. We landed in a ball field at the edge of one town. Instead of the crowd we expected, there was a farmer with a horse-drawn buckboard. This was a two-wheeled vehicle with a board stretched between the two wheels. The farmer had been instructed to take us into town, where a really big rally was waiting. This delay was going to mess up our schedule, but what could we do?

The farmer sat on the left side of the board, I sat on the right and Ruckelshaus sat in the middle, right behind the horse. The horse expelled large quantities of used oats on the way to the rally.

I always told him later that this was the inception of his dedication to clean air.

Ruck Takes a Joke

When Bill was director of the Environmental Protection Agency, he frequently was called to testify before our Public Works Committee.

Once, he was testifying against thermal pollution (the rise in temperature caused by steam from an electric generator being expelled into a river). I had a study that was done by DePauw University that suggested that there was an increase in the number and va-

William Ruckelshaus has that unique combination of ability and integrity.

riety of game fish in the exhaust of these power plants. I asked Director Ruckelshaus if he considered that all these great fish were polluting the river.

Roasting the Ruck

I think Bill Ruckelshaus was one of the most capable and honest men that ever served in Washington. But I always liked to tweak him whenever I could, because he had a great sense of humor and responded well.

During the end of his career in government at the end of 1984, a group of people had a "roast" in his honor. Since I had been working him over and knew him well, I was asked to attend and give him my best shot.

Unfortunately I couldn't make the banquet, but I agreed to be taped on the Capitol steps. Senators Patrick Moynihan and John Heinz had similar scheduling conflicts and also appeared on the Capitol steps.

Moynihan was first. He told how Ruckelshaus was the attorney general who permitted Watergate, how he headed the Environmental Protection Agency, then left to go to work with one of the big polluters, then returned to Washington to clean up the mess he had made, etc. etc.

I was next. I put my hat on crooked, turned up my shirt collar, pulled my jacket down over one shoulder, faced the camera and said: (using my best rural Indiana twang) "Yep, I knowed ol' Bill Ruckuslous. I drive him all around Indiana when he run for Senate or whatever he run for. I'll always remember him. He was a man of few words, but he used them often. He could walk into an empty room and blend right in. Someone said he was modest. Well he had a lot to be modest about. I guess he was a self-made man, which sure is a case of unskilled labor."

I don't remember what else I said about him but when I finished, John Heinz, who was to follow me, laughed and said, "I can't follow that," and walked away.

Bill's Jill

Bill's wife, Jill, was as well-known as he was. She was a very articulate promoter of women's rights and a much sought-after speaker.

Once she agreed to speak at a fundraiser for me in Princeton, Indiana. The night before the event, a man propped a ladder against her window, climbed in, and raped her.

We were all distraught to have such a terrible thing happen to such a super lady. Bill was out of town at the time.

We presumed, of course, that she wouldn't be able to make our fundraiser and I was to "wing it" myself. The next night as the people began to assemble, Jill was one of the first to arrive.

Ed Koch, Neighbor

Ed was a pretty good mayor of New York but I didn't agree with him much when he was in Congress. Congressman Koch was elected in 1968 and was assigned an office next to mine in the Longworth House Office Building. I saw his name on the door and made a neighborly call.

I had no idea where he was from or what his politics were. I have some good friends named Koch (pronounced cook), so I asked for Congressman Koch (Cook). The receptionist was offended. "His name is Koch (Kotch)" she told me, and "what do you want to see him about?"

"I'm your next-door neighbor," I explained, "and just wanted to know if I can be helpful to you as you set up your office. My staff is very competent and would be pleased to answer correspondence or help with your files until you get settled."

She cooled off a bit and took me to see the man himself. When I explained the reason for my call, he became very cordial and thanked me profusely for my offer of assistance. We both got pretty busy then and I didn't see him for a while.

A few months later he dropped into my office and asked me to co-sponsor a bill he had introduced. It was way to the left of my interests, so I thanked him but declined.

A little later he invited me and some of my staff to a party he was having in his office. After we cleaned up our work for the day, a couple of us wandered over. Ed had a bunch of his constituents from Greenwich Village. One look at the long hair, the beads, the strange posters on the wall, and the hint of an odd fragrance in the air and we did an immediate about-face and rushed out. We didn't know what kind of party he had going, but weren't anxious to find out.

My next official contact with Ed was the last. Except for exchanging pleasantries, we didn't have much to talk about. One evening Ed rushed in, grabbed me by the wrist, and shouted, "Come with me." I started out the door and asked where we were going.

"We're going over to the Capitol steps and get arrested for protesting the war!" I was told.

"Just a cotton-picking minute," I responded. "Ed, I want to be a good neighbor, but please don't involve me in of your political activites. Got it?" He got it.

The Congressional Golf Tournament

Back in 1967, some of us thought it would be a great idea to have a golf tournament between the Republican and Democratic members of Congress. The very exclusive Burning Tree Country Club agreed to let us play there.

I was the prize chairman. Jack Anderson wrote of my activities by observing that Congressman Zion, ex-marketing executive, sent out letters to lobbyists, in terms they couldn't refuse, demanding expensive prizes. He said that my office looked like the salad days of King Farouk with TV sets, golf clubs, etc. As usual, Anderson was only slightly correct. He implied that members of Congress could be "bought" by golf prizes.

The truth is that the best prize was a set of Ping irons, donated by the aircraft company that was proposing to build the SST (Super Sonic Transport). The prize was won by the Congressman who was the chief opponent of the SST.

The Burning Tree members were upset by having their club mentioned in a Jack Anderson article, and never invited us back again. We have met every year since then at the Andrews Air Force Base.

The second year of the tournament, Les Whitten, one of Jack Anderson's fellow axe-men called to see if I was to be prize chairman again. A member of my staff told him, "Yes, the Congressman will be chairman for prizes. He has told the members that Jack Anderson will be staked out at 200 yards. Anyone hitting him will automatically win the tournament, plus the undying gratitude of all the members."

Oddly enough, Jack wrote stories about me several times after that, none of which was accurate and none of which was very flattering.

Ford to the Pin

One year when Jerry Ford was President, he played in the tournament. It looked odd seeing men dressed in suits all over the place. The Secret Service men were in the woods, in golf carts, on the course and in the clubhouse.

There was a prize for the player who hit the ball closest to the pin on a par three. I smoked one up real close. A Secret Service man drove up in a golf cart and asked, "Are you going to take the prize? You just aced out the President by six inches!" What a dumb question.

Golf with the Secretary of Defense

In 1988 my partner was Mel Laird, ex-congressman and later secretary of defense under Jerry Ford. We were playing against Representatives Earl Hutto of Florida and Charlie Whitley of North Carolina.

The match was pretty even, but Mel and I managed to win the first nine by a couple of strokes. About that time, helicopters with

My golfing buddies have included (l-r) Secretary of Defense Mel Laird, and Congressmen Earl Hutto and Charles Whitley. That's me on the right. Laird was a great secretary —fair golfer.

public address systems flew over and announced, "Everyone to the clubhouse; dangerous lightning is in the area."

Mel and I thought the match was over, so we settled down with some friends and a martini over a gin rummy game.

After an hour or so, the storm cleared the area and the match was resumed. It seems that Earl and Charlie had been drinking Gatorade and getting charged up for the last half of the match. They clobbered us!

Buddy Hackett—Gun Lover

Once I agreed to help a national gun group by signing up a prestigious panel of advisors. It wasn't a tough assignment because like many issues, most people are on one side or the other and don't mind being associated with their point of view.

One noon, while lunching at the Madison Hotel Grille, I spied the well-known television personality, Buddy Hackett. I introduced myself and asked how he felt about the right to bear arms.

"I'm all for it," he told me.

"How would you like to be on an advisory panel for a pro-gun group?" I asked.

"That's a great idea," he responded. "Everyone should be able to have as many guns as they want. The only thing, though, is we ought to outlaw all ammunition."

Giddy-Up-Gay at the Kennedy Center

When our three children were young they came under the influence of a swim coach named Jim Voorhees. Jim was a fitness fanatic. He practiced a rigorous program of exercise and diet himself, and insisted that his young swimmers do the same. He also instilled in them a fierce competitiveness. It was the greatest thing that could happen to them at a time when children were turned off and were protesting against everything. Our kids were too busy working out to get into trouble.

This conditioning, both mental and physical, helped daughter Gayle and sons Scott and Randy become outstanding athletes.

When Gayle was a small child, she added ballet dancing to her other activities. She earned her name Giddy-Up-Gay as she galloped through McCutcheonville on her horse "Midnight." I can still see her in her tutu and cowboy boots, with her ballet slippers over the saddle horn as she rode to her dancing lessons.

Gayle graduated from Southern Illinois University with honors in physical education(naturally). While she was attending graduate school at the University of North Carolina, I was a member of a subcommittee on Public Works that was considering the building of the Kennedy Center in Washington.

Kenny Gray of Illinois was chairman of the committee. Kenny was an ex-auctioneer and super salesman. He convinced most of the committee that the center would be built by private funds, so they supported the project.

As is so often the case, the private funds weren't adequate, and the argument goes that you just can't let a building die when it is half-finished, so the taxpayers would have to bail it out.

Then there were other problems. Apparently the architects didn't think of the noise that airplanes made as they flew over the center to land at Washington National Airport, so they needed to add a few million extra dollars for soundproofing.

Anyway, the center was eventually finished and the committee members were invited to a big reception celebrating the opening. I called Gayle in North Carolina and asked if she wanted to attend the event.

She packed her sheep dog, Mandy, in a dog crate and the two of them flew up to Washington.

We were assigned a table with some very "artsy" people who were delighted with the beautiful new performing arts center.

They thanked me for supporting it. "Well actually, I opposed the project all along." I explained. "I didn't see why the working people at Whirlpool and Alcoa should have their taxes raised so that people who can afford high-priced tickets can enjoy subsidized entertainment."

"Well!" an over-stuffed lady huffed, looking at Gayle. "What do you think of a father who thinks so little of cultural activities."

Now what this lady didn't know is that Gayle has two things she won't tolerate. One is kids who don't go all-out in athletics and, two, anyone who says anything negative about her family.

I thought for a moment that Gayle was going to crawl across the table and belt her one. Instead she just glared at her with lightning coming out of both eyes and said — very slowly: "I... think...he's...great!!" The rest of the evening was very, very quiet.

Challenging the A.M.A.

Once I was asked to speak to the members of the American Medical Association in Chicago. I urged them to change their image.

"You people are always against everything," I told them. "You should form a committee and introduce some health care legislation. You don't have to settle for socialized medicine but you can promote an insurance plan that keeps the private sector involved."

Apparently they thought it was a good idea, and in a year or so they did recommend a comprehensive plan. It didn't get very far, but I was pleased to be a sponsor.

A speaker who preceded me at the Chicago meeting was Doctor Morris Fishbein. Dr. Fishbein was editor of the AMA Journal and was said to be one of the best informed doctors in the world. He told of a patient who came into his office complaining of a sore elbow. "Try soaking it in ice water." Dr. Fishbein told him.

"Ice water?" the patient asked. "My maid said I should soak it in hot water."

"Well," Dr. Fishbein reassured him, "my maid says ice water."

A Tough Boss

Napoleon: "Take care of your men and they will take care of you."

Most Congressmen know that they can't possibly do the job

alone. They appreciate the tremendous job that the loyal, dedicated, hard-working staff does for them.

Of course there are as many management types in Congress as there are in business.

Not all bosses are loved by their employees. One member I knew was known for the turnover of his staff people.

He loudly criticized them in public and seldom had anything good to say to them. He gave his press secretary an especially tough time. Though he never went over any of his speeches that were written for him beforehand, he always complained about them after he delivered them. He insisted that they be written out completely on a large type machine so that he could read them without his glasses. The press secretary decided that he wouldn't take the abuse any longer and wrote one final speech.

The Congressman was at a podium before a large audience of his constituents. After the applause died down, he began: "Ladies and Gentlemen, I am delighted to be with you this evening. Never before have we had such important events to shape our lives and the lives of our children and grandchildren. There are four very critical subjects that I plan to discuss this evening. They are..." Then he turned the page.

On the second sheet in very big type was written: "OK, big shot, you're on your own."

Claude Pepper Matriculated on Campus

Claude Pepper of Florida was once a great orator. When he served in the Senate he was known as President Roosevelt's trial balloon flyer. When Roosevelt wanted to try out an idea, he would ask Claude to make a speech on the subject. If it was accepted, the President got behind it; if not, he dropped the idea.

An opponent of Claude's once made a speech in which he accused: "Are you aware that Claude Pepper is known all over Washington as a shameless extrovert? He is also reliably reported to practice nepotism with his sister-in-law, and he has a sister who was once a thespian in Greenwich Village. He has a brother who is a practicing homosapien, and he went to a college where men and women openly matriculated together. It is an established fact that Mr. Pepper before his marriage practiced celibacy. Worse than that, he has admitted to being a lifelong autodidact."

Gitmo Cuba

My first experience with Claude was a trip to Cuba in 1967. The U.S. has a large Naval base at Guantanamo Bay. It has been

there for many years under a contract with the Cuban government. Under the contract the Navy base hires many Cuban citizens for non-military duties and buys water and electricity from the Cuban government.

Castro, in a fit of pique in late 1966, decided to cut off the water supply to the base. Someone on the Public Works Committee in Washington thought it would be a good idea to float a desalinization plant down to the base and distill sea water. The base would not have to depend on Castro for water. A committee of Congressmen was selected to fly down to the base and decide if it was a feasible plan.

We flew down in a large four-engine prop Navy plane. The situation with Castro was not too good at the time and some of the members were a bit on edge. As we approached Cuba, fighter planes suddenly appeared on each side of our transport. I was playing gin rummy with Jack McDonald of Michigan when he spotted the one on our side of the plane closing in fast. I thought he was going to dive under the seat, and I wouldn't have been far behind him. Fortunately our pilot came on the intercom and announced that these were U.S. Navy fighters and that they were escorting us to the landing.

When we arrived, it must have been 100 degrees and very dusty. We were assigned rooms in barracks where we put on sports shirts and baseball caps. Everyone but Claude Pepper, that is. He did take off his jacket, but he kept on his homburg hat.

Our first mission was to tour the island by Jeep. Claude and I were in the third or forth Jeep. As we rode down the very dusty road, the dust boiled up and covered us from head to foot. I can still see Claude sitting there in a very dignified and erect position with that formal hat. He looked like a tan snow man.

We drove to a high hill overlooking the bay, where our Navy guides offered us some field glasses. As we looked across the bay we saw some Cuban soldiers looking at us with their field glasses. Apparently they do this all the time. The Americans on one side and the Cubans on the other. In the middle was the Navy fleet bobbing at anchor in Guantanamo (Gitmo) Bay.

We all noticed how easy it would be for Castro to lob bombs down on the U.S. ships and fervently hoped it wouldn't happen.

Some of us took a military helicopter gun ship and flew around looking at the Cuban military installations. They were doing the same. It was a cat and mouse game with each side suspicious of the other.

Leaded Fish

After our tour of the island, some of us went fishing in the Admiral's barge. It was a good-sized fishing boat, well equipped and suitable for eight or ten fishermen. We each put two dollars in a hat. The money was to be split between the man who caught the most and the one who caught the largest fish.

After a couple of hours, we headed for the Admiral's residence where we could weigh our fish and split the reward. It was fairly obvious that I had the largest one, but we had to go through the drill of weighing anyway.

I was standing on the front deck as we started in. For some reason I glanced into the pilot house. There was Cliff Enfield, minority counsel of the committee, stuffing lead weights into his fish. When we docked, a Naval officer was standing by with a fish scale. Mine was weighed first. Just as Cliff offered his for weighing, I grabbed it by the tail and gave it a good shake. The weights fell out, everyone had a good laugh, and I collected my booty.

Electricity, Too

The trip was a success. In addition to making the base independent of Castro for water, we also authorized an electric power plant. In the process of distilling sea water, a lot of steam is released. We thought it would be a good idea to use that steam to turn a turbine and run a generator.

So, as we returned to Washington, we were satisfied that we had done the job we were sent to do.

Codel Klu

In 1968, some members of the Public Works Committee were asked to attend an international road federation meeting in Beirut, Lebanon. I had heard that if you want a great congressional tour, you should go with John Kluczynski, the chairman of the Roads Subcommittee. "Big John" always carried a bag full of Kennedy half-dollars and handed them out to everyone he met in foreign countries.

He was from Chicago and kept his watch set on Chicago time, wherever he was. Incidentally, Kluczynski liked Polish stories. Like the time the Polish army bought a bunch of septic tanks but couldn't find anyone to drive them.

He liked to tell about a Congressman who came to the committee for funds to help with a pollution problem in Lake Michigan. It seems that a fish called the alewife was dying by the hundreds and washing up on the beach. This discouraged tourists, who are big business in that area.

One suggested solution was to import the Coho salmon to the lake. The Coho had voracious appetites and would devour all the little alewife, grow to a big size and increase the fishing potential for the area. They tried this but found that the Coho absorbed pesticides and the health department said they weren't good for human consumption. So back to the drawing board. It was discovered that the walleye pike from Minnesota was immune to pesticide infiltration so they crossed a coho with a walleye. The resulting fish was lazy. It wouldn't put up a fight and didn't rise to the fishermen's bait. One last try was to cross the coho/walleye with a muskie, the big fighting fish from Wisconsin and Minnesota. It worked! They finally created a cross between the coho/walleye and the muskie.

They called it the cowalski...but they couldn't teach it to swim. Big John made many speeches in which he promised, "as long as John Kluczynski is around, no one will touch a dime of the interstate and defense highway money for anything but the national highway system."

Unfortunately, Chicago Mayor Richard Daly had a different idea. He ran Chicago politics with an iron fist and personally decided who would run for Congress and what he would do when elected. He asked KIu to take some money out of the highway bill for use in a cross-town highway through Chicago. Poor John had to comply.

He came to my office, and also to other members of the committee, and said with tears in his eyes that, "Ol' John had to go back on his word." It wasn't long after that that Johnny Klu died and we lost a great guy.

A Zion in Beirut

When Kluczynski's delegation arrived in Beirut in 1968, it was obvious that, even then, there was a lot of tension. Most of the anxiety was caused by Arab-Israeli problems, but the American Embassy had been fired on. Everyone was on edge.

When we checked into the hotel, Kluczynski was assigned a room, Jack McDonald had no problem, committee counsel Cliff Enfield got in, and so forth, but when I told them my name was Zion, I thought they were going to duck under the desk. I tried to explain that I wasn't a Zionist, that my name was German, but they still couldn't seem to find my reservation. Fortunately, the American ambassador to Lebanon was Dwight Porter from my district in Indiana. He convinced them that I was not a threat to their lives and they let me in.

The International Road Federation meeting was convened to study highway safety methods, road construction techniques, information signs, etc. Highway builders from all over the world attended. It was a very productive meeting. Beirut, in those days, was the vacation area of the Middle East. One could go snow skiing in the mountains in the morning and water skiing in the ocean in the afternoon. There was a huge nightclub on a hill overlooking the city that rivaled anything Reno or Las Vegas could offer. We saw the most spectacular act we had ever seen. It involved six white horses on a huge treadmill, galloping at top speed toward the audience. The horses were pulling a sleigh with a female driver. She was snapping a whip over their heads. Johnny Klu observed that if anything happened to that treadmill, we would have tons of horses in our laps.

Belly Dancer's Pawn

One evening a young diplomat from the embassy agreed to show McDonald and me around the town. He presumed that we would want to go to a nightclub and see belly dancers. Now Jack and I, of course, were the epitome of decorum. Our young guide, however, sipped a few cocktails at a reception and became a bit aggressive.

When he was told that the nightclub was sold out (lots of road builders in town) he told them that he was hosting some V.I.P.s and demanded a table. They set up a table for three right on the dance floor, where we not only had a great view of the dancers, but became part of the act.

During one swirling number that involved a long pink veil, the dancer concluded her number by draping the veil over my head.

The next morning at the meeting, a road builder from Milwaukee came up to me and announced that he had taken a great picture of me at the critical part of the dancer's act. He further mentioned that he was anxious to give a copy to my father when he returned to Milwaukee. Now my father was a very conservative Boy Scout executive in Milwaukee. I wasn't sure how he would react to seeing his Eagle Scout son bedecked in a thin veil next to a semi-clad belly dancer in Lebanon. He never mentioned it.

McDonald Missed the Six-Day War

After the road federation meeting a few of us took a side trip to Israel. We checked in with the American Embassy and were assigned a hotel room. Early the next morning I was awakened by a military attache who was taking me to a golf game. McDonald slept in.

I expected this. While we were being entertained by the young man in Beirut, he confided some interesting information. We were told that when a congressional delegation is to arrive at a foreign post, the State Department sends a message telling them what to expect.

For example, he told us that if one of the Kennedys was coming, they should expect a big interest in women and booze. I asked him what they had told him to expect from McDonald. He sort of hesitated and then diplomatically suggested that Jack shouldn't prove to be a problem and had no outstanding requests. When Jack asked him about me, he was more explicit: "He's an athletic nut; keep him busy."

Our golf game was at the only course in Israel. It was half way between Haifa and Tel Aviv. We played with the U.S. air attache and the head of the Israeli air force. It was a peculiar golf course, built in the middle of a desert. It looked like someone with a large sprinkling can walked around. Wherever he walked there was grass. Everywhere else was sand. Some giant bushes were clustered around, too. If a ball went into these bushes it was lost. No one went looking for it.

I don't know if it was because it was a frivolous search or because there were poisonous snakes in the bushes. Maybe both. During the golf match, and the small reception that followed, one thing was obvious. The Israeli air force was very well trained, very much on edge and very anxious to take a shot at the Arabs. The slightest excuse was all they needed.

When I got back to the hotel, I found that McDonald had spent most of the day at a beach. The next day we went back to Washington. I told my press secretary that the Middle East was about to explode and she used that as a headline for a story that we released.

McDonald wrote a story predicting peace in the Middle East. Two days later the Israeli air force attacked and started the vicious Six-Day War. I took my hawkish story down to Jack's office and taped it to the top of his desk.

The Ugly Americans Visit Europe

In 1973, McDonald and I took a trip to Prague, Czechoslovakia. The official reason was to study their unique highway construction techniques. The unofficial reason was to check out a Czech colonel who was suspected of being a double agent.

McDonald, somewhat of an international jet-setter, had met him sometime in the past and, it was hoped, could find out where his sympathies lay.

When we arrived at Prague we were met by a young man from the American Embassy in an embassy car. This was shortly after the Russians had moved in and shot up some buildings at St. Wenceslaus Square.

We were curious about the Russian presence in the country and asked our guide lots of questions: "How many Russian troops are in the country? Where are they? Have they held any Czechs captive?" Every time we asked a question, our guide changed the subject. It didn't take us long to realize that he either didn't know anything or wasn't going to answer if he did.

When we got to the embassy we were asked up to the ambassador's office. The embassy was in a huge castle in the heart of Prague.

Before he'd hardly acknowledged our presence, the ambassador motioned for us to follow him. We went up a long, winding, stone stairway to a big room. In the middle of the room was one of the darndest things I've ever seen: A conference room enclosed by plastic floor, walls, and ceiling. In the middle was a conference table and about a dozen chairs. We went through a plastic door and sat around the table. "I'm sorry if we seemed rude," the ambassador apologized, "We presume that everyone in town is a communist spy, and we don't talk about anything we don't want them to know. We know that the embassy is bugged, that our driver is probably a double agent, that your hotel room is bugged and that you will be followed wherever you go. The only place in town where we can communicate is in this plastic room. You can see that there are no electronic devices here."

He then told us all about the Russian influence and how the local Czechs tried to confuse them. They changed the street signs, painted anti-Russian graffiti on the walls, changed the mileage signs and generally tried to make them feel confused and unwelcome.

The next morning we were met by the colonel suspected of being a double agent. He was very polite, exceedingly hospitable, and,

I thought, unusually curious about our visit. Jack explained that he just wanted to see him again and that we were anxious to see some of their public works projects.

We saw the sights and played the role of visiting Congressmen to the hilt. The colonel took us on a good field trip. I have always been fascinated with castles. On a trip to a new road project, I noticed that there was a beautiful old castle that was available for tourist visits. We asked our driver to take us up to see it. The car had to stop about two hundred yards short of the castle because the road was too steep to drive. As we climbed up, it was obvious that these beautiful stone towers were built for defense. An attacking army would have a big disadvantage with the castle defenders able to shoot arrows and throw rocks and hot oil down on them.

We had enjoyed some Czech beer at lunch and hadn't made a pit stop since. The first part of the tour involved a short lecture about the history of the castle. While we were waiting to hear the talk, Jack asked our driver to find a restroom. The guy was gone for about five minutes and came back with a satisfied look on his face.

"Did you find a rest room?" Jack asked.

"Yes, thank you," he replied.

One evening the colonel and his wife took us to dinner. Apparently she didn't speak a word of English, which seemed odd since the colonel was very fluent. As is usually the case, a young American diplomat and his wife went with us. Later we learned that when the two women went to the ladies room, the colonel's wife chatted in perfect English. When we got back to the hotel it was rather late in the evening. Jack and I told our hosts that we were very tired and thought we would turn in.

After about a half hour, we peeked out the door of our room and didn't see anyone. It was our plan to visit some Prague nightlife undetected by our ever-watchful hosts. We had been walking down the street for a few minutes when we heard a band playing. We couldn't help but feel smug because we had given the secret police the slip and were out on the town just like any native Czech.

We went into the nightclub and were assigned a table. Up to now we hadn't said a word that would give us away. At least, so we thought. Before we could order anything a young man came to our table and planted an American flag right in the middle. The band played Yankee Doodle. So much for our incognito visit to Prague's nightlife. When we got back to Washington, we had a two-hour debriefing with military intelligence. We had kept careful notes. We told them about everyone we saw, where we went, etc. They were especially interested to note that the colonel's wife spoke English. To this day Jack and I don't know what we accomplished, if anything. The debriefers seemed delighted with the information we had collected. We learned a lot about the fate of people who are under the heel of an occupying army.

The *Christophoro Columbo*

Since we were on vacation, we had planned to take a circuitous route back to the States. Being interested in transportation, we took a train down through Italy, expecting to meet up with the Italian cruise ship *Christophoro Columbo* for the voyage back toNew York. As we settled back and listened to the clickety-clack of the wheels, we wondered why the U.S. couldn't support a better rail system. It wasn't long before we had some reservations about the Italian system. Suddenly the train stopped. We looked out the window and saw an orange orchard. Soon we saw the train crew sitting under the orange trees eating lunch and drinking wine. We thought that was a bit odd and asked Cliff Enfield, our committee counsel, to check it out.

He came back with some disturbing news. It seems that the crew was on a strike and it was unlikely that we would make our port in time to embark on the cruise. Now McDonald is a man of action. He took off toward a distant farm house, but we didn't see how he could communicate with the natives, nor what he could accomplish if he did.

We should never have underestimated our man Jack. Somehow he had managed to contact the American Embassy, requesting a car to rush us to the port. He also called the ship and asked the captain to hold up departure until we got there. We unloaded our suitcases at a road near the train and sat on them, waiting for the embassy limousine. It didn't arrive. Instead of a large car, the embassy sent a small Volkswagen. There was no way we could get ourselves and all our luggage in that small car.

While we were trying to decide who/what should take the car and who/what should be left behind, the train whistle tooted and the train started to move.

Jack and I had bought some fancy Italian shoes in Rome and were wearing them. As we chased after the train, throwing our bags onto the platforms as they chugged by, we completely ruined them on the crushed rock road bed. When we got to the ship, a host of disappointed passengers was lining the rail, waiting for the ugly Americans.

Though the departure was only delayed by an hour or so, we were *persona non grata* for most of the trip to New York.

Panic In Panama

In 1968, a group of congressmen was asked to help dedicate the Pan American Highway. One of Lyndon Johnson's poker buddies was the Ambassador from Panama and was instrumental in getting U.S. funding for the project. Naturally, the top majority members of the Public Works Committee were involved. Senators Jennings Randolph and Steve Young represented the Senate, and John Kluczynski represented the House.

Since they always want to show bi-partisan support for these international pork barrel projects, they invited minority members Bob McEwen of upstate New York and me to go with them. It was a disaster from the beginning. We arrived at the airport and were entertained by some Panamanians who thought that congressmen drank before the official cocktail hour. They supplied some gooey sweet drinks at the airport and on the plane too. As we were letting down to the airport at Panama City, I shoved my seat back and knocked McEwen's drink all over him.

As all good flight attendants know, a little carbonated water cleans you up pretty well, so when we landed, McEwen was a bit damp but otherwise in not too bad a shape. We were assigned a limousine with a driver and host. Though they didn't speak very good English, they gave us the impression that there was a big party to celebrate our arrival and that we were to check into a hotel first.

McEwen thought, what the heck, why don't we go straight to the reception and check in later. That was apparently O.K. with the driver so we headed for a convention hall. As we arrived, a band played, hundreds of people cheered the rich Americans, and the festivities began. There were great toasts and welcoming speeches.

Half-an-hour later, heads of our delegation arrived and found that all the welcoming ceremonies were over. They were obviously and bitterly disappointed. The next morning, we were driven to the Panamanian president's house for breakfast. It was a bit disconcerting to see men with machine guns in trees on the way to the President's house and also standing on the roof where we arrived.

We were told that there were only two big families in Panama and they were constantly feuding. Each wanted the presidency and the spoils that went with it, and they fought each other for the job.

After breakfast, we were driven to a school. Bob and I didn't have any idea why we were there. We presumed that our delegation leaders knew what was going on but they didn't feel it was necessary to clue us in.

There was a chain-link fence around a courtyard and a spread of food on long tables. Bob observed that the temperature was in the low hundreds and that the food was covered with flies. Nonetheless, when the gates were opened, a throng of people rushed in and started devouring everything in sight. Bob and I stood around, nibbled on an apple and wondered what in hell we were doing there. I was getting hot so I retreated to our limousine, where the driver was waiting with the motor running and the air conditioner on high.

When I got into the back seat, there was a very attractive young lady sitting there. I thought "When did that sly dog McEwen line her up?" I certainly was surprised by his action but I did admire his taste.

She said something to me but all I understood was that her name was Raquel. In a few minutes McEwen showed up and was as surprised to see the young lady as I was. I've always been flattered to think that he credited me with the "conquest."

Raquel spoke to the driver and we were off. We drove for a couple of hours and finally arrived at a Panamanian summer resort called Boquetti. Raquel invited us to meet her family, but the driver seemed pretty upset and we declined.

We left Raquel at the resort and drove at break-neck speed toward Panama city. (In retrospect, we concluded that this woman wanted a free ride to see her parents and we were convenient pawns.) When we arrived at Panama City, we were taken to a fire house where we were expected to freshen up and change for dinner. A man (apparently the fire chief) ran up to us and tried to tell us some exciting story. A woman (probably his wife) kept shaking her head "no" all the time he was making his presentation.

"He wants us to do something and she doesn't," I commented. "What should we do?"

"How should I know?" McEwen answered with a shrug.

While we were debating what we were supposed to do, the fireman brought out his new engine, It was now apparent that he wanted to show off with his new prize (probably bought with U.S. funds). With a clang and a wild siren he brought the engine out of the station and hooked it up to a hydrant. Then he grabbed a hose and turned on the water. It was obvious that this was not a one-man operation. The hose knocked him down. Like a huge python, it coiled and uncoiled and shot water all over the place. We all got soaked. As we went up to the firemen's quarters to change clothes, the fire chief's wife was giving him a lecture. We didn't have to understand Spanish to know what she was telling him.

Of course we were late for the big celebration. This was the second welcoming banquet in two days. This time Randolph, Young and Kluczynski were on time and McEwen and I were late. The next day was the official dedication of the highway. We got up early, had breakfast and were assigned limousines to drive to the site. The first car held the Panamanian officials and Senator Randolph. The second had some other dignitaries and Senator Young. The third was for Kluczynski and some staff people. Bob and I were in the fourth one. We drove down some narrow, winding roads through a dense jungle. The temperature must have been at least 110 degrees.

When we arrived at the spot where the highway was to start,

native people seemed to materialize from the jungle all around us. There were women nursing their babies, men with machetes, half-naked children and old people. We had no idea where they came from or how they knew we were going to be there.

Now the real trouble started. Jennings Randolph, who was quite elderly and overweight, got down from his limousine and started walking to a makeshift speaker's platform under a galvanized metal roof. He took about a dozen steps and collapsed. Steve Young, even more elderly and weighing only about 140 pounds, tried to pick him up. He too collapsed. John Kluczyinski, also in his seventies and very heavy, sat down on a rock and turned ashen.

The Panamanian leaders ran around like a bunch of nuts. McEwen and I tried to offer some help but we weren't feeling too well ourselves. The transition from the air-conditioned limousines to the hot, humid jungle was too much for these Washington parlor-pansies. Besides, we had been wined and dined to excess. Eventually some helicopters flew in and took Randolph, Young and Kluczynski to a hospital. That left me and McEwen to handle the task of officially dedicating the start of the Pan American highway.

Great! We didn't have the speeches, we didn't know Spanish, we felt lousy, and we wished we hadn't come in the first place. Finally we were ushered up to the platform, which was even hotter than it would have been without the tin roof. The Panamanian officials made very long speeches and Bob and I tried to smile when it seemed appropriate. At last the ceremony was concluded, and we were driven back to our hotel.

By that evening, our senior celebrities had made remarkable recoveries and were ready for another banquet. This time, they had their speeches. Oh how we wished that they hadn't! We had heard, but not understood, many long speeches. Besides, McEwen insisted that his kidneys couldn't stand another day of bashing. He observed that when these people wanted to show appreciation, they gave you an "embrasso." This is sort of a hug but with an exaggerated pat on your lower back. McEwen said that the next guy who gave him a kidney punch was going to get it right in the nose. At last it seemed that everyone in the house had made a speech about this great inter-American project. So to make everything complete, they introduced me. At least I think they did. They looked at me as they mispronounced my name. I had had it!

Though I'm sure very few people understood me, I told them that I had a serious lack of highways in my own congressional district; that I was desperately trying to get funds for Interstate 64 across Southern Indiana; and that until we finished the interstate and defense highway system in the U.S. I wouldn't vote for one dime for the Pan American Highway.

It was suddenly very quiet. Finally the silence was broken by thunderous applause... from McEwen. Our relationship with some members of the delegation was a bit strained for the rest of the trip. Bob and I sort of liked it that way. When I got back to Washington, the whole expedition came to a conclusion I might have expected.

While I was gone, a thief broke into my apartment at the Capital Park and stole my valuables, a woman down the hall had been murdered by a laundry man, and I had a notice about a rent increase. Oh! It was great to be back.

Mom and Curtis LeMay

My mother thought that people who worked and saved their money should live better than those who didn't. She also thought that the government shouldn't spend money it didn't have any more than taxpayers should. During the Depression, when Dad cut his own salary so he wouldn't have to cut back on the pay of his two assistants, my mother took in a roomer and served breakfast to him and a man who roomed next door.

Years later my folks moved to a retirement community in Laguna Hills, California, when Milwaukee got too cold for my Dad and they fit in very well. Most of that congressional district in California was made up of retired business people who felt as she did. The district was appropriately represented by a John Bircher named John Schmitz, an ultra right-wing ex-professor from Santa Ana College.

He could have stayed there forever if he hadn't crossed President Nixon. In 1974, Schmitz thought that Nixon was too liberal and ran against him for president. When Nixon made diplomatic approaches to China, that was too much. Schmitz made a speech one day while Nixon was in China, saying that he didn't mind the President going to China, but he wished he wouldn't come back.

This didn't go well with the residents of Leisure World and the surrounding area. They thought of the President as a neighbor at nearby San Clemente. They voted Schmitz out of office.

During a lame-duck session of congress, Schmitz gave a farewell talk to the prayer breakfast group. During the question period that followed, he was asked if his district was really one of the most conservative in the country. "Conservative?" he asked - "I've got John Wayne, Curtis LeMay (head of the Strategic Air Command), and Roger Zion's mother."

During one of his more relaxed moments, President Richard Nixon meets with me in his private living room prior to a reception. I presented him with a souvenir of the U.S.S. Indiana.

Chapter Six

Of the Presidents I have known, Richard Nixon was the hardest to understand. I just didn't know what to make of him. I really think he was sincere in what he wanted to do, but was a bit awkward socially.

Nixon came to Evansville once to give a speech for me. We met him at the airport and had a police escort to Harrison High School where he made his talk. He did a good job, said all the expected nice things about me, and left with me for the airport. As we were getting into the car, he said, "Now Roger, sit by the window, smile and wave, smile and wave."

I did as I was told, but somehow it all seemed a bit fake and unnatural for me. Nixon did it well.

One Saturday I was making a speech for a political rally at a hotel in Princeton, Indiana. As I concluded my remarks, the mayor of the town (who also owned the hotel) came up to me. He was visibly excited. "Mr. Congressman," he almost yelled, "the White House wants you to call right away."

I was rather excited myself. Since I was chairman of the task force on energy resources, I thought that the President wanted me to go to the Middle East, or come to a special conference on the subject. The mayor lived a block down the street from the hotel.

"Come call from my phone," he implored. "It's just down the street." I later learned that he had a bronze plaque installed on the wall by the phone. It read: "On this day September 17, 1973, President Richard M. Nixon talked to Congressman Roger H. Zion."

So I did call the White House. When the woman at the switchboard answered the phone, she was expecting me. "Just a minute Mr. Zion," she said. "The President wants to talk to you."

Now I was really excited. "Hi Roger," the President greeted me. "What are you doing working on your birthday?"

He did a lot of personal things like that.

One day Esther Bray, wife of Congressman Bill Bray of Indiana, was recovering from surgery in a Bloomington hospital. While she was still in the recovery room, she received a call from President

Nixon. He just wanted to know how she was doing and wanted to express his concern.

He always sent personal contributions to my campaign. Long after Watergate, he still keeps in touch with his old friends. He has written three books, *Real Peace, Leaders,* and *Memoirs of Richard Nixon.* He has sent each of them to me with personal notes. I think he is really a caring man but he just got a little carried away and trusted his two political hatchet-men (Erlichman and Haldeman) too much. He let them play hardball against his political opponents when it wasn't necessary. Then he, because of a strong feeling of loyalty, covered up for them when they got into trouble.

I Don't Introduce Dole

After Watergate, the Republican Party was in disarray. My district had a predominantly Democratic registration. Many Democratic friends had to cross over and vote for me or I could never have been elected. It appeared that they would revert back to their own party by November. But, life goes on and the Vanderburgh County Republican Party planned a big Lincoln Day fund raiser. I often said that everything that ol' Abe was when he moved to Illinois (advertised as the Land of Lincoln), he became as a youngster in my district of Indiana.

He lived on a farm near Gentryville. So we made a big deal out of Lincoln Day and usually collected enough money to pay the central committee bills for much of the year. One problem was that it was difficult to find a big name speaker to "fill the hall." The committee chairman called me in Washington and asked me to help. Poor Bob Dole was national chairman at the time and felt obligated to fill in when no one else would take the assignment. Bob is a good friend of mine and one of the nicest guys I have ever known. He is also one of the funniest. It was difficult to get a chair near him in the House cloakroom (while he was a member) when he delivered his usual humorous comments on the passing scene. Bob agreed to be our featured speaker and we set a date.

Unfortunately for me, the day that the big event was scheduled

If it weren't for his great sense of humor, I don't think Bob Dole could put up with being a permanent minority party leader.

President Jerry Ford addresses a White House meeting of former members of Congress.

Bill Simon wore many hats in Washington, but never that of President. Too bad—he would have made a great one.

also was a day that the House was in session. I had an almost-perfect voting record and told the committee that I couldn't make the event. "Oh, you have to come!" they insisted. "There will be two thousand people there. They will expect you and, besides, you must introduce Dole. Like a nut, I finally agreed to show up and in the process, pounded a nail in my political coffin.

Here's the scene: Two thousand cheering people, in spite of Watergate. A high school band providing atmosphere. All the party faithful hoping for a lift from the daily depressing news. The national chairman to speak.

The county chairman takes over and introduces practically everyone in the house—all the visiting county chairmen, the state candidates, the local candidates, the rally chairman, his committee, the former office holders, etc. Some wag once commented that they introduce everybody but the salt shakers.

Then I get introduced. I'm to make a couple remarks and then introduce Dole. I get tremendous applause! As is my usual procedure, I reach into my jacket pocket and pull out a 3x5 card on which I had written some funny remarks about my friend Bob Dole.

Just as I start to speak, the county chairman taps me on the shoulder and whispers "Keith Bulen will introduce Dole." T h e r e is a pause—a long one. L. Keith Bulen was our national committeeman and had come down from Indianapolis.

As our official state representative to the national committee it was natural for him to introduce our national chairman. I just wish someone had mentioned it to me before I got up in front of two thousand people with Dole's introduction in my hand.

I was stuck. What to do? What to say? The only thing that came to mind was our national tragedy: the Watergate break-in. I made up one of the stupidest statements I have ever uttered and one that would follow me around forever.

"We are all concerned about Watergate," I proclaimed. "Well, let me tell you something. It was a very simple breaking-and-entering for which the perpetrators should get a suspended sentence. The Watergate break-in was just a prank much less serious than all the sabotage and dirty tricks that went on by the Johnson campaign people. If you ask me, the whole thing is blown out of perspective by a vicious press, anxious to sell papers or increase ratings."

Well, there was some cheering and some applause... none of it from the press table right in front of me.

From that day on, every time I was mentioned by the media it was "Roger Zion, who justifies Watergate," or "Zion, Nixon's greatest booster," etc. It was not a popular image in 1974.

Tapes Did Him In

At the peak of the Watergate fiasco in August 1974, I got a call from Chuck Wiggins, Congressman from California. Chuck was recognized, on both sides of the aisle, as an authority on constitutional law. He wanted me to meet with him and a few other people, to plan the defense of Richard Nixon during impeachment proceedings.

When I arrived for the meeting, a few House members were there, as was Barry Goldwater and Hugh Scott. Scott was the ranking Republican senator and Goldwater was one of Nixon's best defenders. Wiggins wasn't there.

We waited for a half-hour or so and Wiggins came in. He looked terrible. Though normally tanned, his face was ashen. He fumbled for words. Finally, he said, "Rather than planning for the President's defense, we must select a committee to go and ask him to resign.

"I have just heard the White House tapes. I don't think we have any defense at all."

Wiggins, Goldwater and Scott called for an appointment and left for the White House. The next day, Nixon made his resignation speech.

Ku Klux Klan

Indiana was a great state for the Klan. My Dad remembered seeing parades of mounted Klansman with white sheets on the riders and their horses. He insisted that most of the Klansman were Evans-

THE WHITE HOUSE

WASHINGTON

February 20, 1974

Dear Roger:

The joint letter you signed recently
urging me not to resign the Presidency
has been received and I am grateful
for this expression of sentiments by
you and your colleagues in the House.

It is my intention to remain on the
job and perform my duties in the best
fashion possible. As I endeavor to
fulfill my responsibilities, it is
reassuring to know that I have your
support.

With kindest regards,

Sincerely,

The Honorable Roger H. Zion
House of Representatives
Washington, D.C. 20515

When I received this letter from Richard Nixon, neither of us realized that his days in the White House were numbered.

ville mounted policemen.

Though the Klan isn't what it used to be, it still has some numbers and occasionally stirs up some action. During the 1974 campaign, the grand dragon of the Klan was interviewed on a local radio station. He was asked what the Klan was. "It's a patriotic organization" he responded. "We hate Blacks, Jews, and land-grabbing Catholics."

"Why don't you have a candidate for Congress?" he was asked.

"We like Zion, that's why," he answered.

I didn't get many endorsements that year, but that was one I could have done without. The guys at the radio station enjoyed that statement so much that they played it at least a dozen times.

Scum Bags Who Have Known Me

The local media people thought it was time for a change in Congress in 1974 and they expressed that opinion editorially. The most enthusiastic endorsement I have ever seen for a political candidate was written in 1972 by Gordon Hannah, editor of *The Evansville Press*. He urged the citizens of Southern Indiana to re-elect me.

Gordon left *The Press* in 1972 and was replaced by Mike Grail, who didn't like me very much. One of the most damaging editorials was one written against me in *The Press* in 1974. I hadn't changed, but the newspaper had.

The worst example of really dirty journalism was a job done on me by John Dancy of NBC. He phoned and asked me if he could spend a day with me during my campaign. I said, "Sure," so he came down to Evansville.

It couldn't have been a better day if I had written a script. The day started with a breakfast meeting with a senior citizens group. I explained some programs that would be helpful to them. Several of them had problems that they told me about. I took notes and arranged to help them by contacting the appropriate government agencies.

Next I went to a shopping center where I handed out literature. A former teacher of mine came up, told me what a great job I was doing in Washington, and helped me hand out the brochures. Several people came by and thanked me for the casework I had done for them.

Next I had a luncheon meeting that went well. I answered a lot of tough questions and showed that I knew what was going on in Congress.

In the afternoon I visited a school, gave the children a flag that had flown over the nation's capital, and gave them an inspiring talk about the importance of education.

All of this time, the cameras were turning and their sound was on, and the reporters were getting a terrific picture of a well-known, hard-working Congressman doing his job. The NBC camera crew recorded the whole story.

I couldn't wait to see how this played on the national news. When I saw it, I couldn't believe it. John Dancy's voice was narrating a sad story about Southern Indiana. He told of how there was much unemployment and showed pictures of padlocked plant gates. He showed poor people sitting around in messy surroundings, and told of how depressed the area was. Then he showed a picture of me standing in front of a supermarket and said something like: "People in Southern Indiana are very unhappy with their representative in Washington. Next November they will do something about it."

The manager of the local TV station that carried the bit called me and apologized. It was a bit late.

Jack-Ass Anderson

I had frequently read Jack Anderson's column in a local newspaper. I presumed that he probably stretched a point to be sensational and used colorful expressions to confuse and mislead his readers.

Shortly after arriving in Congress I read an article in which Anderson said that Congressman John Buchanan, a swinging ex-Baptist minister, had hired a mini-skirted former *Playboy* bunny and Adam Clayton Powell reject to work in his office.

Sounds bad, doesn't it? What is implied here? Well, "ex-Baptist minister" sounds like he was kicked out of the church. "Swinging" implies that he led a very active extra- curricular social life. "Adam Clayton Powell reject" sounds as though the young lady in question had worked (or socialized) with the former chairman of the Education and Labor Committee who was found guilty of criminal activity and tossed out of Congress.

Now the truth is that John Buchanan was still a Baptist minister, though he was serving in Congress. He worked very hard, was a credit to his church, and had no social life at all except that required for his job.

The young lady had never worked for Powell. She had been a talented entry-level staffer on the Education and Labor Committee on the minority side and had never seen Powell. Buchanan, who was a member of the committee, needed a secretary and she was hired.

On my first day on the Public Works Committee, the ranking minority member, Bill Cramer of Florida, moved that all meetings of the committee be open to the public. The chairman has the discretion of holding closed "executive sessions" if he choses. All Democrats voted against the notion and all Republicans supported it. Because we were outnumbered, the motion to have all meetings open failed.

Later I asked Cramer what that was all about. "Why should Jack Anderson be the only one who knows what goes on in our executive sessions?" he answered. It seems that Anderson had a mole on some of the key committees who filled him in on what happened in secret committee sessions. I don't know if they were paid by Anderson or if they were protected from his vicious pen by acting as informants for him. I do know that people like Anderson are not encumbered by the truth.

An example of his mole at work was evident one day when we were called in to an emergency meeting of our committee. It seems that a dam had broken in West Virginia and the resulting flood had caused some serious damage.

When I got to the committee room, I asked a representative of the Army Corps of Engineers if the dam had been built to federal specifications. He answered that it was a local dam built to prevent mine spoils from getting into a fishing stream. I observed that we should insist that these dams be built to protect people. Jim Wright of Texas, who later became Speaker of the House, agreed that people were as important as the environment. At this point Jim Key, a representative from West Virginia, came into the room and asked for a review of what happened. He wanted to be brought up to date.

This is a paraphrase of how Jack Anderson reported the meeting after getting the details from one of the members:

Yesterday in a behind-the-scenes rump session (doesn't that sound ominous?) some members of the Public Works Committee who give lip service to the environment met to tear up environmental laws. Roger Zion of Indiana said environmental laws are ridiculous and silly. Jim Wright of Texas, with white teeth flashing, snarled "to hell with fish." Dim-witted Jim Key of West Virginia didn't even know what was going on.

This kind of derogatory journalism is the main reason that Congress gets a low rating from the public. In this case, the proper committee of Congress met to help solve a particular problem. We investigated it and offered legislation to prevent the problem from happening again. Jack Anderson completely misinterpreted the whole procedure.

Truckers Buy a Congressman

Once in 1974, Anderson wrote that the American Trucking Association came to Washington with its pockets full of money. When it left town, Congressman Zion of Indiana introduced a bill to help big trucks and tear up the nation's highways.

The truth is that Lieutenant Governor Bob Orr of Indiana called me and asked if it would be possible to increase the size of trucks in interstate commerce so that companies like Whirlpool and Alcoa could ship their products more economically. We held hearings on the subject, during which witnesses testified that larger trucks posed no increased danger to motorists and larger trucks could have better brakes that could help them stop quicker. Witnesses also testified that one could get many more refrigerators or air conditioners in a slightly larger truck. I introduced the bill.

Scripps-Howard newspapers circulated a cartoon showing a big hog named Zion eating up a highway. They argued profusely against the bill and it failed.

The American Trucking Association lobbied for the bill but they (in contrast to Anderson's implication) didn't pay me a dime. Partly in jest, I frequently brought this to their attention.

I once talked to some White House staff people who were maligned by dirty journalists and asked why they didn't sue the *!?#'s. Since I was seriously considering a suit against Anderson, I was especially interested in what they had to say.

It appears that people in public life are easy targets for the poison-pen pushers. I have been told that people in public life should have thick skins and expect criticism. In order to get satisfaction from the courts a person in public life must prove: 1. That the columnist lied. (That's usually easy.) 2. That the writer did so with malicious intent. (That's a bit more difficult.) 3. That the suer suffered some specific damage as a result of the false story. That means that one must prove that he lost his job, lost his income or suffered other measurable loss as a result of the scum bag's story. We read of celebrities getting huge settlements from sensation writers. Compared to the number of damaging stories that are written are the tiny number of victims who get satisfaction.

40,000 Feet and No Parachute

Charlotte Reid was a very charming and talented representative from the Chicago area. Her husband had been a candidate for congress while Charlotte was a vocalist on Don McNeal's breakfast show. Mr. Reid died during the campaign and Charlotte was drafted to take his place. She was elected and re-elected many times.

Once she came over to me on the House floor and asked if I would go with her to Chicago to speak to a Young Republican meeting. It seems that she had lined up a private jet and Tricia Nixon for the trip but needed an additional speaker to fill the bill.

One of her staff people drove us to the airport, and we met with Tricia. I had met Tricia previously and knew her to be a very vital and beautiful young lady and a definite asset to the Nixon family.

We were well on our way to Chicago, when smoke started to fill the cabin. The copilot came back and said that a fire had broken out in the electrical system and that we were turning back to Washington. Trish said, "Hey! We're halfway to Chicago. We can reach there as easy as Washington. Let's go for it."

So we did. On the way, the copilot extinguished the small flame and, because of Tricia's gutsiness, we got to the meeting and didn't disappoint several thousand Young Republicans.

Rails Visits the Today Show

Tom Railsback of Illinois was elected with our big group in 1966. Tom had been a very big man-on-campus in Illinois. He was a bit liberal, compared to most of us, but he was sincere about it. I tried to talk him into voting a more conservative line but couldn't budge him.

I even told him that he would get defeated by a more conservative candidate but, again, he stuck to his convictions.

Once Tom was invited to appear on the "Today" show to promote his idea that delegates to the Republican National Convention be a microcosm of the United States. He strongly felt that the Republican Party needed to reach out to everyone. His own voting record showed that he supported the labor unions, increased welfare, higher minimum wages, more government involvement in the social system, etc.

On the evening before his big TV appearance, House Minority Leader Bob Michel and I went to dinner with Tom to try to persuade him to take a less strident approach to the subject.

We tried to explain that there would be no need for two political parties if both of them had the same philosophy. We stressed the difference between the two parties. We told him that the Republican Party appealed to people who wanted less government and more independence. We told him that Republicans want to work, to build factories, to provide services, to hire people and to earn money. Democrats, we told him, want to spend the money that Republicans earn.

"Rails" left us and went to his apartment to get a good night's sleep.

Bob and I thought about our discussion and the need for "Rails" to present differences between the two parties. In order to continue our argument we decided to wake him up and convince him of the error of his ways. So we did. We kept ol' Tom up 'till way after midnight.

Though we didn't make him change his story, we did make him look mighty sleepy and less convincing at the early-morning TV show.

"Rails" is a good golfer and a longtime member of the Burning Tree club where he has played with Jerry Ford, Bob Michel and other celebrities. One afternoon in early 1991, "Rails" and I were playing Burning Tree. It was getting late in the evening and we were rushing to finish before dark. As we putted out the seventeenth green we heard a "fore" from way back on the seventeenth fairway. Just then a ball rolled up the green. Rails hollered, "You *#?!! Hold your horses!!" We finished and were posting scores and chatting with the men in the pro shop when the perpetrator of the golfing "no-no" came in.

"If I had known it was you two characters, I would have hit it harder," said our good friend, Vice President Dan Quayle.

He was finishing up a fast eighteen holes as the guest of Secretary of Transportation Sam Skinner.

Jean the Dream

John Ashbrook served eleven terms in the House. I sat next to him on the Internal Security Committee and knew him to be an unusually dedicated conservative who sincerely tried to oppose what he considered to be ultra-liberal threats to the American political system. His contribution to the process was cut short in April of 1982. John was running for governor of Ohio when he suddenly died of gastritis.

In a special election his wife, Jean, was elected to represent his district. Jean really added a spark to what is sometimes a dull and

Jean Ashbrook tried to be everything to her constituents that her late husband, John, had been. Too bad she wasn't re-elected.

stuffy Congress. She was bright, attractive, and friendly, but a bit naive.

She wanted to be "one of the boys," and gathered with us at the Capitol Hill Club after work. The club is a convenient place to wind down and talk politics and legislation. Even though I was no longer in Congress by then, as a consultant with a Washington office, I spent (and still do) a lot of time with members—including at the club in the evening.

Guy Molinari of New York took it upon himself to walk Jean to her apartment and generally protected her from the evils of the District of Columbia.

One evening, we decided to walk down the street to Bullfeathers for a hamburger.

Jean didn't know it, but Bullfeathers was only a few hundred yards down the street from the club.

As we left the club, there was a chauffeur-driven limousine at the front door. High-level government officials and wealthy dignitaries frequently stop by the club, and it isn't unusual to see a limousine out in front.

Molinari guided the new Congresswoman to the big car, opened the back door and ushered her in. He then closed the door and strolled on down the street.

The driver looked around, saw the attractive blond passenger and didn't say a thing.

After a brief wait, Jean wondered what happened to our group. Finally it dawned on her that she had been the subject of one of Molinari's pranks. With great dignity, she alighted, saw us standing down the street laughing, joined us, and we went for a hamburger.

Once Molinari worked very hard for an appropriation for a Coast Guard installation in his district. When it was approved, Senator Alphonse D'Amato sent out a press release announcing the grant and, in effect, taking credit for it.

Molinari was steamed and tried to reach D'Amato on the phone. He was told that the senator was attending a convention. Not to be deterred, Molinari called the convention center and told the phone operator that he was the commandant of the Coast Guard and needed to talk to the senator immediately. He was patched through to the meeting room and gave the senator a good dressing-down.

A little later (as reported in *The New York Times*) D'Amato was interrupted again by a call "from President Reagan." He grabbed the phone and yelled: "Damn you Molinari, leave me alone!"

"Hey, Al," Reagan said. "I need your help with an appropriation bill that is before your committee."

The Great Put-Down

Even though I'm no longer in Congress, I still have access to the House floor, dining room, and gym, and I still participate in a weekly Congressional Prayer Breakfast. I've also continued playing on a congressional bridge team. In the few times that members can get away, we play in tournaments.

Kathy Wei, world champion player, helps us when she can and does a great job promoting the American Contract Bridge Association. She got the idea of a charity match between the "money makers" and the "law makers" in May of 1989.

Kathy, who is chairman of the Falcon Shipping Company, knows a lot of prominent people. She called Malcolm Forbes, the multi-talented publisher, balloonist, motorcyclist, friend of Elizabeth Taylor and great bridge player (He has since died). Between them they lined up a team which included some of the most powerful men in America. Their team included Warren Buffett, now listed as the second wealthiest man in America; Larry Tisch, chief of CBS and chairman of Loews Corporation; and Alan Greenberg and James Cayne, chairman and president, respectively, of Bear Stearns companies. Greenberg was also a member of the Board of Governors of the American Stock Exchange. This team also had Jack Dreyfus of the Dreyfus Fund; George Gillespie III, lawyer and director of *The Washington Post*; and Milt Petrie, CEO of Petrie Stores.

An interesting aside is the story of how Jimmy Cayne was hired as an account executive with Bear Stearns. On his application he mentioned that he was a life master bridge player. Alan "Ace"

149

Greenberg fancied himself a pretty good player, too. In an interview he asked Jimmy how good a player he was. Jimmy answered, "Mr. Greenberg, if you played for the rest of your life you wouldn't be as good as me."

Jim got the job and he and "Ace" have played in international tournaments ever since.

The congressional team consisted of me and Congressmen Arlan Stangeland of Minnesota, Robert Kastenmeier of Wisconsin, James Leach of Iowa, Howard Nielsen of Utah, and Lynn Martin of Illinois. (Lynn Martin later became Secretary of Labor.) The Senate provided Hank Brown of Colorado, Robert Packwood of Oregon, Robert Kerrey of Nebraska, and Rudy Boschwitz of Minnesota. One of our coaches was Mel Wells, a Washington judge.

The match was held at the Capitol Hill Club in Washington. Corporations bought ads in the program and kibitzers paid to watch. Proceeds from these funds were donated to Barbara Bush's charity, Reading is Fundamental.

The Carlton Club

The British Parliament challenged us "colonists" to a match in London later in 1989. The House of Lords and House of Commons have had competition for years, but our team can seldom get together to practice. Kathy Wei offered to come to Washington any time to coach us before the match, but the one time we asked her to come, only four of us showed up. So we were overmatched and got beat.

We had a terrific time though. The Duke of Marlborough was a member of the British team and invited us to lunch at Marlborough castle.

The big event, however was Thanksgiving dinner at the Carlton Club just prior to the match. Now this is probably the most exclusive club in the world, and certainly the fanciest.

The foyer is impressive with lots of dark wood paneling, huge oil paintings of famous members, a long stairway, and gorgeous draperies. A bomb meant for Maggie Thatcher once killed some

This is the Congressional team that played the "Money Makers."

very important people at the Carlton Club, though Maggie escaped.

Tom Petri, a member of our team from Wisconsin, started to take some pictures. A very tall, very thin, very British gentleman in white tie and tails came up to Tom, stuck his nose in the air and said "One doesn't take photographs in the Carlton Club."

The match itself was held at the Park Lane Hotel in Piccadilly. Our team consisted of Congressmen Arlan Strangeland, Gerry Solomon of New York, Hank Brown, Petri, Lynn Martin, Jeff Stafford of Virginia, and me. Judge Wells filled in for a missing member.

We played six boards consisting of four hands each. The U.S. team was leading until the last hand, when Solomon inadvertently played a king of diamonds (stuck to a low heart), and the British made a small slam to win the match. We mention this to Solomon often!

Post-Tournament Fling

After our defeat at the hands of the British Parliament, we were invited to a formal dinner dance on a large party boat on the Thames.

A trophy was presented to the winners, and many speeches were made.

I was selected to be the emcee for the colonists. Introduced our members, each of whom had a funny story to tell or a song to sing. We all sang "God Bless America," and our team captain, Arlan Stangeland of Minnesota, sang "Oh It's Hard to Be Humble (When You're Perfect in Every Way)."

After we had exhibited our unbridled enthusiasm, I heard one Lord say to another, "Those Yanks are so happy, you'd think they'd won."

Jack Kemp—President?

In 1980 Beurt SerVaas, publisher of *The Saturday Evening Post*, called me and asked me to write an article about Jack Kemp. Beurt was convinced that Jack had all the attributes of a great President. I agreed.

The article started: "The spunky quarterback faded back and threw a desperation pass down the field. Mac Speedy, wide receiver, ran under it and into the end zone. The Buffalo Bills won the championship and Jack Kemp proved to be an all-pro quarterback and big time winner. He has been a winner ever since."

In the article I told of how truckers all over the country would carry Kemp for President signs from coast to coast because of legislation he had introduced. I talked about Jack's Kennedy-like appearance and natural appeal. I mentioned his economic theories and how appropriate his remarks were for our point in history.

It was a great pitch and would have been very impressive if it had ever been printed.

Unfortunately, SerVaas went on an African safari shortly after asking for the article and met John B. Connally of Texas.

I remember that shortly after Connally was appointed Secretary of the Treasury, he spoke to a Republican caucus. We usually had cabinet members meet with us every other month or so. It gave them a chance to plug for their favorite programs and gave us a chance to know them better and ask questions.

The cabinet member usually brought two or three assistant secretaries and books of figures, charts and other back-up material.

When Connally showed up, he came alone with only a smile and a clean handkerchief in his breast pocket. Though he had been in office but a few weeks, he knew his agency from stem to stern and answered every question with great authority.

I remember turning to Al Cederberg of Michigan and saying, "Either this is the smartest man I've ever met or the biggest con man." It turned out that he was one of the smartest and most articulate men I've met.

Anyway, during their safari together, Beurt changed his mind and ran a big article about John Connally instead of Jack Kemp. That helped Connally decide to enter the race.

John Connally didn't make it to the presidency, but he showed his appreciation for our efforts, nonetheless.

Wearing a cap to protect my bald head from the sun, I sample food at the annual congressional golf outing, which pits Democrats against Republicans. It's a highlight of my year.

Connally's Delegation

Shortly after the *Post* article, Beurt and his wife Cory SerVaas had a reception for John and Nellie Connally in Indianapolis to kick off his campaign. They asked me and Dave Dennis, also of Indiana, to attend.

At the reception, Connally asked me to help in his campaign and be a substitute speaker for him when he was not available. I agreed. My old classmate George Bush had written from China and asked me to help him, but I was so impressed with Connally's oratory that I thought he might be a better candidate. One day I asked Congressman Bill Archer of Texas who he thought would have the best chance of winning in Texas, Connally or George Bush. He didn't hesitate a second. "Oh no!" he told me, "You're not going to get me in the middle of that controversy. John and George are both good friends of mine, we are members of the same country club in Houston, and I'm not going to show favoritism for either one."

Connally hit many states and raised a whole lot of money. Bob Dole, George Bush and Ronald Reagan weren't doing nearly so well in the early days of the campaign. I once asked Bob Dole to help me with an issue that was coming up in the Senate. "Why don't you ask John Connally to help?" he suggested. I didn't know that my very small participation in the Connally campaign had come to his attention.

By the time of the Republican convention Connally had raised a lot of money but had signed up only one delegate. It has been said that John had more money per delegate than any other candidate in history. Boy! Can I pick 'em.

Senator Archer?

Toward the end of 1981, there was a rumor that President Reagan was going to ask John Tower to resign his seat in the Senate and accept the position of Secretary of Defense.

Texas Governor Bill Clements would be faced with the opportunity of appointing an interim senator until the next election.

Congressman Bill Archer and I were cooling down after a paddleball game in the House gym when the phone rang. It was Bill Clements asking for Archer. He wanted to appoint Bill to the senate seat if Tower resigned.

"If I take the senate seat, will I have any opposition in the next primary?" Archer asked.

"I'll get back to you," the governor responded.

About five minutes later the phone rang again. It was Bill Clements saying that Jim Collins of Dallas was interested in running and would, in fact, oppose Archer in the primary.

"Thanks, but no thanks," Archer told him. Tower wasn t asked to take the job at that time, but Collins ran and was defeated by Lloyd Bentsen, and Archer continued to win overwhelmingly in his House seat.

Oh, Yeah

Jim Ford, the House chaplain, started his career as a small-town preacher in Minnesota. He served as the chaplain at the military academy at West Point for several years and was then elected to his present job as chaplain of the House.

He was at West Point when the Bicentennial was being celebrated. He and a friend wanted to do something spectacular, so they bought a small sailboat, had it shipped to England, and sailed it across the Atlantic to New York. Jim says it really tested their faith on several occasions but they made it across.

Apparently they kept each other company by telling all the jokes they had heard. Ford's favorite was about some preachers who met for coffee each Monday morning. One of them was upset because he had lost his bicycle and couldn't remember where he left it.

Another clergyman had experienced the same problem a year earlier. He said he solved it by preaching the Ten Commandments for his Sunday sermon. He made special mention of "Thou shall not steal." A day later his bicycle was returned.

This seemed like a great idea, so the first preacher took theTen Commandments as his subject the following Sunday. When he got to, "Thou shalt not commit adultery," he remembered where he left his bicycle.

Hudnut's Greatest Hour

After Watergate, it was apparent that Republican chances were considerably diminished. The 1974 re-election prospects of those of us who swept in because of Lyndon Johnson's unpopularity in the mid-sixties, were threatened by the drop in public opinion that Nixon was suffering.

Spiro Agnew was a big hit on the lecture circuit and his expressions like "The Nittering Nabobs of Negativism" and "pusillanimus pussyfooters" got a lot of press coverage. He was, at that time, one of the greatest fund-raisers of all time.

The Indiana delegation got together and agreed that first-term Congressman Bill Hudnut of Indianapolis, was in danger of being defeated. Since Agnew could only make one speech in Indiana, we agreed that he should help Bill.

Both John Myers and I felt that we weren't in danger but that Andy Jacobs, whom Hudnut had defeated, would be a tough competitor.

We further decided that we would have a "Hudnut Day" in Washington to boost his candidacy. To make it especially helpful, we named Hudnut, "Hoosier Legislator of the Year."

We had some friends fly out "roastin' ears" and barbecue from Indiana. We engaged a special room at the Georgetown Inn and invited the Indianapolis news representatives to attend; of course we also invited Hoosier celebrities too.

On the special Hudnut night, we drove out to Georgetown and started the festivities. Dick Roudebush, who headed the Veterans Administration, gave a glowing report about Hudnut's contribution to the State of Indiana. Agriculture Secretary Earl Butz gave a similar tribute. Max Freidersdorf, chief White House aide, did the same thing.

The media folks were drinking it all in. It was great! — Except that when Hudnut started to stand up and accept the honors, he pushed down on the round table edge and turned the whole thing over. All the food, beverages, glasses, etc. spilled all over him. It was quite a sight.

Anyway, it ended well. Hudnut got a lot of well-deserved publicity to help him in the coming election.

The only trouble was, he got beat. So did I. So did Bill Bray, David Dennis, and Earl Landgrebe. We started 1974 with seven Republicans in the Indiana delegation and ended with two.

Communists, Who Cares?

In 1974, because of my work on the Internal Security Committee, I was asked to address the National Meeting of the American Legion in Houston, Texas. It was a great assignment.

Our committee's staff members had infiltrated the peace movement, the Communist Party USA, the gay rights bunch, and the Socialist Worker's Party. As actual working members of these organizations, they had the names of subversive individuals who were working against the U.S. government. I decided to go all-out and identify these people by name and organization. It was a risky business but I felt it should be done.

The committee made several reservations for me under different names so that I could avoid being intercepted. Indiana Governor Ed Whitcomb sent a squad car and two state troopers to watch over me. They reserved the room next to mine in the hotel and followed me everywhere.

At the time of my speech they escorted me to the podium. I did my job. I named names and kicked asses. The Legion loved it.

After the meeting was over I decided to dine in style and invited the troopers to go with me to the Houston Petroleum Club; a very ritzy club on the top floor of an office building.

I was a member of the Evansville Petroleum Club and assumed that I could bill my club for the check. When dinner was over, I handed the waiter my card. "That's no good here," he told me. I didn't have enough cash for the bill so I asked what I should do. "You can bill it to one of our members," the waiter told me.

An historic photo of Indiana's congressional delegation: It was the last time the delegation was dominated by conservatives. Gov. Ed Whitcomb is the tall guy in the middle. He is flanked by (l–r) John Meyers, Elwood "Bud" Hillis, me, Bill Bray, David Dennis, and Earl Landgrebe.

Addressing a national meeting of the American Legion in 1974, I identified individuals and groups subverting the U.S. government. The audience loved my speech, but the general public didn't seem to care that the peace movement was being controlled by Communists.

I thought a minute. "Is Congressman Bob Casey a member?" I asked.

"He sure is," was the reply.

"Well, just bill it to him," I suggested.

I really didn't know Bob Casey, other than to see him on the House floor. He was a lean, stern-looking Texan. I didn't know how he would take this.

As soon as I got back to Washington, I called his office. When I talked to the staffer who handled his checking account, I pleaded with her to let me know as soon as his Petroleum Club bill came in. I planned to rush over and pay her.

A few days later, Casey came over to me on the floor. I didn't know which to do first, duck, or reach for my wallet. "I hear you were my guest while you were in Houston," he told me. "Yes, I was and I'm sorry, but I didn't know any other Houston Petroleum Club member so I stuck you with the bill. How much do I owe you?"

"Not a cent," he replied. "I was honored that you thought of me. Please be my guest any time you are in Houston."

How 'bout that!

We didn't want to send out press releases prior to my speech because we didn't want to alert all the subversives in advance. So we sent them out immediately afterward. It was assumed that this revelation with specific names and organizations would be big-time news.

My press secretary bought a special scrapbook to handle all the newspaper articles that covered the monumental event. We didn't need it. Except for a nice Page Two story in the Vincennes *Sun-Commercial*, no one else thought it worthy of notice.

My only memento is a bronze plaque which hangs on my office wall. It has an American Legion symbol at the top and it reads, "Americanism citation awarded to Hon. Roger H. Zion, courageous congressional defender against atheistic Communism and terrorism."

Someday maybe a grandchild will see this and say, "Wow! Pop must have been some guy."

Back-Room Politics

Once I got a call from a prominent committee chairman who asked me to meet him at the "horseshoe" at 7:00 the next morning. (The horseshoe is the name given to the driveway in front of the Rayburn House Office Building.) "What's going on?" I asked.

"I can't tell you," he responded.

"Why should I come then?" I asked.

"You'll see when you get there," was his reply.

I was at the appointed place and time and found two other Congressmen there, too.

We were picked up by an unmarked station wagon and headed south. No one said a word during the trip that ended up behind the Pentagon, the world's largest office building.

We were escorted through endless corridors to the office of James Schlesinger, the secretary of defense under President Nixon.

It seems that the Secretary was concerned about the sale of some computer parts to the Soviet Union. He was convinced that they could be put to military use. The Secretary of Commerce and the Secretary of State apparently didn't share the concern and were lobbying the President to permit the trade deal to go through.

Schlesinger didn't want to cause an interdepartmental fight over the issue so he wanted us to take the whole subject to the general public. He convinced us that he was right, so we all made speeches on the House floor and sent out news releases expounding the evil that would result if these computer parts were sold to the Russians. Eventually we won the argument and the back-room politics served a useful purpose.

The Pizza Express

Once I got caught in the Dayton airport with then-Senator Dan Quayle and Representative and Mrs. Carroll Hubbard of Kentucky.

We had arrived from Washington and had to change planes in

Dayton for the flight to Evansville, Indiana. Piedmont cancelled the flight to Evansville.

We called Washington; we tried to reach a private pilot from the Tri-State Aero in Evansville to come get us, but nothing seemed to work.

Quayle was scheduled to give a commencement speech in Evansville and Hubbard had one in Hopkinsville, Kentucky. It looked as though they weren't going to make it.

I asked the hostesses in the Piedmont lounge if they had any friends who flew private planes. "Hey! I know the pilot of the Domino's Pizza plane," one of them exclaimed.

"Give him a call," I suggested.

He was at the hangar. We got a ride over to the hangar and took off in a small plane with a domino painted on the tail.

Dan Quayle made his speech in Evansville, and Hubbard and his wife were flown in the "Pizza Express" to his Kentucky meeting.

I don't know about Hubbard and Quayle, but since that hitch-hiking ride, I have been partial to Domino's Pizza.

The Huggers

In 1989, I was on a plane heading for Washington when I struck up a conversation with a seatmate, a holistic physician. I had never heard of one. She explained that holistic physicians are medical doctors who treat the whole patient. This includes medical, surgical, psychological, and spiritual treatment.

When she found out I spent a lot of time in Washington as a legislative consultant, she said she wished that members of Congress understood what holistic medicine was all about. I suggested that she have a reception, invite all the members and have a spokesman for the doctors explain about their specialty.

I was already attuned to the concept because I had read *How to Live 365 Days a Year,* by a Dr. Shindler of the Monroe Clinic in Monroe, Wisconsin. In his book, he documented the fact that 80% of all illness results from E.I.I., which he described as Emotional Induced Illness. If that is true, then certainly psychiatry and religion must play a large part in therapy.

I volunteered to set up a reception for her group, not really expecting she would take me up on the offer. But, in a week or so, I got a call from a young lady in Virginia who said she was the secretary of the National Holistic Medical Association. She wanted to come into town and help me arrange for the reception.

I told her how to get to the Rayburn House Office Building and said I would meet her there. Everyone was very helpful. The catering people, the police who let her park in front of the building, and the Speaker's office, which arranged for the meeting room. Since I was no longer a member of Congress, I had everything put in Congressman Gene Snyder's name and charged to his bill. Of course, he was to be reimbursed by the Holistic Society.

To put it mildly, the secretary was most impressed by the treatment she received.

As we were leaving the Rayburn Building after making all the arrangements, she turned to me and asked, "Do you hug?"

I was a little surprised, but not enough so that I didn't stand there in the Rayburn patio and vigorously hug in front of quite a throng.

In a couple of days I received an article in the mail from a medical journal that was written by Dr. William A. McGarey. It was entitled, "Hugs Better than Drugs." It explained in detail the therapeutic effect of hugging. He said that his people start every meeting by hugging. A final word in the article said, "Four hugs a day are necessary for survival, eight are needed for maintenance, and twelve are needed for growth."

If this is true, most of us are many years in arrears on hugs.

The day of the reception, I dropped into Gene Snyder's office to tell him that he was hosting a big reception and suggest he stop by and say, "hello."

"Who am I hosting?" he asked.

"A national hugging society," I replied.

"A what?"

I told him again.

"Sure. Sure it is," he mumbled, with a bit of doubt in his voice.

"Come on," I urged. "You won't have to stay long."

Well, we walked in the door and I told the holistic doctors that Congressman Snyder had arranged the reception, and—you guessed it—they all took turns giving him a big hug.

He'll never doubt me again.

Snyder was elected in 1962, lost with the Goldwater election in '64, and was re-elected in '66. His campaign manager was an engineer named Bill Tanner. Tanner agreed to come to Washington and help set up his office and then return to his home in Kentucky. As so often happens, he kept moving back his retirement date and stayed until Snyder retired in 1988.

The Congressman went back to his district every weekend to visit constituents. Tanner drove him to the airport and kept his car until Gene came back the following Monday.

Congressional cars have a prominent sign in front signifying the driver is a member of Congress.

One Thursday, Gene and Bill were on the way to the airport when Snyder observed that they were early and suggested that they stop at a tavern for a beer. "Naw—let's don't," Tanner complained. "We might be late."

Snyder insisted and, being the boss, prevailed over Tanner's objection.

When they walked in the door, the bartender waved and shouted at Tanner, "Hi, Congressman Snyder! What'll it be?"

Snyder liked to tell derogatory stories about people from Indiana, especially when I was around. He claimed that Indiana people were Kentuckians on the way to Chicago who went broke.

He was full of witicisms. When John Tower was trying to rid himself of all past criticism in order to be approved as secretary of defense, Snyder had this to say: "Anyone who would agree to give up women and booze to take a temporary job is too stupid to handle it."

Incidentally, Barry Goldwater said, "If they threw everyone out of this town who had shacked up with someone else or gotten drunk, there would be no government."

Snyder, Fashion Plate

Snyder wasn't always the best dressed member of Congress, though his wife, Pat, looked like a model.

One day Gene walked up to a member on the floor who was a bit mismatched. He had on plaid trousers, a figured tie, striped shirt, and a jacket that obviously didn't go with any of the above. "Could you come over to my house for dinner tonight?" Gene asked.

"Well, I guess so," the member responded. "Why do you ask?"

"My wife thinks I'm a terrible dresser," Gene told him, "and I want her to take a look at you."

Whoops, Wrong State

John Buchanan of Birmingham, Alabama was a bit too liberal for some of his Republican constituents. Several of us warned him that, like Tom Railsback of Illinois, he should expect a rival conservative Republican candidate to give him some trouble.

In 1980, we were proved to be right. Conservative groups supported Albert Lee Smith against Buchanan, and Albert Lee won the nomination. One of the groups that helped him was the National Rifle Association. Albert Lee was a vigorous opponent of gun control.

In the heat of the campaign, Smith got a phone call from the N.R.A. "We have printed and distributed thousands of 'Albert Lee Smith for Congress' bumper stickers. The bad news is that we sent them all to our members in the wrong state."

It was like getting a kidney transplant from a bed-wetter.It wasn't all good.

Pickle-Hymn Authority

The regular congressional prayer breakfast is one of the highlights of my week. The differences of opinion often expressed with enthusiasm on the floor are forgotten. The members meet for fellowship, to get better acquainted, and to hear the personal history of each speaker.

The program consists of an opening prayer, the reading of a passage from the Bible, the singing of a hymn, and an address from one of the members.

Just before we sing the hymn, Jake Pickle of Texas tells the history of the hymn. He is an authority on church music, though chaplain Jim Ford sometimes wonders if he makes up some of his comments.

Jake will say something like: "This hymn was written by an organist from Hamburg in1827. He had just lost his mother and his father was sent to an asylum. In his grief he suddenly thought of the words of this hymn and he composed the music to go with it."

One day, with my tongue firmly in cheek, I interrupted Jake just before he gave his history of the day's hymn.

"If the gentleman will yield," I asked, "I will explain the origin of this hymn. I'm personally aware of the author because he came from my district." Jake looked surprised and started to protest, but I continued. "This was written by the trombone player of the Salvation Army band in Darmstadt, Indiana. His wife had left him to go off with a traveling salesman, his daughter had taken up residence with a local house of commercial affection, and he was in the depths of despair. Suddenly, he picked up his trombone and this tune just came out."

Jake shook his head. Half the members looked as though they doubted me. I looked at Chaplain Ford. He was nodding in agreement. Neither Ford nor I have admitted that we conspired to twit Pickle with this little bit of drama. We do think, though, that Jake is now a bit more careful with his facts.

During a big public flap about members passing rubber checks in the House bank, the Sergeant-at-Arms, Jack Russ, was asked to write letters for members reporting that they were not guilty of the offense.

Jim Ford announced that the chaplain's office would be pleased to write letters for members who were without sin.

The Big Endorsement

There is a round table in the Members' Dining Room that, by custom, is only inhabited by Republican Congressmen and Congresswomen. When I first came to Washington, I was told that the elderly waiter who served that table was a slave who was personally freed by Abraham Lincoln to wait on Republican members. I've never let facts get in the way of a good story, so I've repeated it a few times.

One day in 1989, I got to sit next to Millicent Fenwick, the pipe-smoking member from New Jersey. Millicent was a good, capable, effective member and didn't deserve the cartoon treatment her character received by Gary Trudeau.

When I say I "got to" sit next to Millicent, I mean that she usually ordered a small decanter of wine and usually drank half of it. Her table partner was offered the other half.

Millicent was thinking of running for the Senate seat in New Jersey, and was seeking encouragement. Dick Richards, chairman of the Republican National Committee, came in and sat at the table next to us. "Is that Dick Richards?" Fenwick asked me.

"Yes, haven't you met him?" I asked.

"No, but I would like to," Millicent replied.

"Dick, I want you to meet our representative from New Jersey, Millicent Fenwick," I told him.

Dick graciously got up, came over and extended his hand.

"A real pleasure," he assured her.

"I'm thinking of running for the Senate seat in New Jersey," she explained, "What do you think of the idea?"

"I'm sure you would be a great candidate," he assured her.

She seemed pleased and asked her friends around the table what we thought of the idea. "Fine," "Good," "Go for it," etc., were our responses.

So she did. She ran against Senator Frank Lautenberg and was defeated. That ended her career.

Wilbur Mills

Wilbur Mills of Arkansas was probably the greatest legislator of our time. As chairman of the powerful Ways and Means Committee he influenced every tax bill that came out of Congress. He was so knowledgeable and well-respected that his word was law.

When the committee brought a tax bill to the House floor, it may have been three or four hundred pages long. Wilbur stood in the well of the House and explained it, title by title.

If anyone had a question, Wilbur answered it. It might take several hours, but Wilbur did a thorough job of covering the entire piece of legislation.

Unfortunately, Wilbur was an alcoholic. One morning at the prayer breakfast meeting, he explained his problem.

It seems that as a young lad he delivered bags of sugar from his father's store to the backwoods stills of the Arkansas moonshiners. They let him sample their product.

Later, whenever he was caught with nothing to do, he took to drinking. He said he kept a bottle of vodka in his refrigerator. He would start with a jelly glass of vodka and not stop until the bottle was empty.

At one point he was sent to Bethesda Naval Hospital for consultation. The Chief of Staff told him he was an alcoholic and had to abstain completely. As is often the case, Wilbur denied it and even called the President to see if he could get the chief fired. The President confirmed that the diagnosis was correct and counseled Mills to take the doctor's advice.

Unfortunately he felt he could take-it-or-leave-it and had frequent bouts of drunkenness. On one of these occasions he met a nightclub dancer named Fanne Foxe and that ended his career.

That was the night he was carousing with Fanne when she took her nationally publicized swim in the Tidal Basin near the Washington Monument.

It also started the usual quips in the cloakroom. Unfortunately, Wilbur's wife, Polly, broke her leg in a totally unrelated accident, about the time of the Tidal Basin excursion. The joke was that a staffer knocked on her door and told her that Mills was in big trouble. He then was supposed to have said, "We've thought of a good alibi, but first we have to break your leg."

As a result of the adverse publicity that the Fanne Foxe episodes created, Wilbur was replaced as chairman of the Ways and Means Committee by Al Ullman of Oregon. Al didn't have the same control over the committee that Wilbur did and there was a lot more floor activity under Ullman than Mills. Members offered more amendments that they wouldn't submit under Mills, because Mills wouldn't permit them.

I remember a big tax bill that Ullman brought to the floor in 1975 or 1976, after I left office and was visiting the House floor. Al was up front pushing for passage. Wilbur was standing behind the rail in the back of the House chamber, smoking a cigarette. Smoking isn't permitted on the floor, but it is presumed that if you are behind the rail, you are technically off the floor. I think he had been drinking.

"How many votes do you think he'll get, Mr. Chairman?" I asked him.

"Oh about eighty or ninety," Mills responded. When the tally came, Mills was right in the ball park. Many people said that Wilbur Mills drunk was smarter than any sober member on the floor.

Wilbur decided to retire from Congress and didn't seek reelection in 1976. He finally recognized that he had an illness and became a member of Alcoholics Anonymous.

I asked him if I could write his story for the *Saturday Evening Post*, and he agreed. He wanted to fight alcoholism any way he could, and felt the story would help. *The Post* published the story and called attention to the terrible effect that alcohol can have on a person, his job, and his country.

When I last saw Mills, he was practicing law in Washington. He and Polly were devoting half of their time and half of their resources to helping alcoholics stay straight. Wilbur had become a nationally recognized speaker on alcoholism.

A great legislator became a great positive influence over something other than the taxing policy of our government. Wilbur died of heart failure in early 1992.

Rank Has It

Once I was making a speech on Mackinac Island in Michigan. Since I had a few hours off the morning of the meeting, I called the tennis pro shop and scheduled a court for 10:00 a.m.

When I arrived at the proper hour I was told that the court had been given to someone else. Now, when someone preempts a member of Congress, by golly, there will be some fur flying.

I waited by the court to see who the hell had bumped me. When they arrived, I understood: Governors George Romney of Michigan and William Scranton of Pennsylvania showed up.

I knew them both and we exchanged pleasantries. I'm sure they didn't know that the pro had given them preference or they would have asked me to join them. Anyway, a governor outranks a congressman anytime.

The next time I was bumped, I was an ex-congressman. I had reserved one of the two indoor courts at the Washington Navy Yard. When I arrived, I was told that the court had been given to the Secretary of the Navy.

Had I been a sitting member, this wouldn't have happened. But as an "ex-con," I was outranked. Rank hath its privilege.

Leave 'Em Laughing

One of my good friends in the Congress was Manual Lujan from New Mexico. He and his wife, Jean, decided that they had enjoyed about as much of being in Congress as they could stand, and were giving it up. He "retired" from public service in 1988 when George Bush was elected.

Manual had been the ranking member of the House Interior Committee, and Bush wanted him to accept the post of Secretary of the Interior. After saying no twice, the Lujans bowed to the persuasive President and agreed to stay around for four years.

As Secretary of the Interior, everything he did made someone violently angry. If he moved to protect the spotted owls, the lumber people, and everyone who depended on lumber, wanted to hang him. If he protected the lumber industry, he got threatening letters from people associated with environmental groups. Poor "Manny" couldn't do anything right.

It reminds me of when Cliff Hardin was Secretary of Agriculture. His first speech was to a farmers' group in Iowa. Their chief complaint was that corn prices were too low and they couldn't make any money. They demanded that he do something about it. His next speech was to the cattlemen's association in Kansas. They complained that corn prices were too high and demanded that he do something about it.

We had a retirement party for the Lujans at the Capitol Hill Club. We asked the chef to prepare their favorite foods, mostly Mexican dishes. We had a small combo playing Hispanic music, and invited the Lujans' many friends to attend.

When the buffet was offered, it was a thing of splendor. Manny had brought some name tags to identify the many exotic dishes. As we trooped through the chow line, we filled up on such delicacies as "spotted owl hash," "bald eagle stew," and "barbecued California condor."

The Lujans were happy to leave all the controversy behind and try to resume some semblance of a normal life.

Me and Clinton? No Way!

Each year, members who work out in the House gym have a banquet. It's a big affair. The men who manage the gym put on suits and ties and serve beer and wine. We start with shrimp, crab legs, smoked salmon, cheese and the like, followed by steak and winding up with apple cobbler and ice cream.

It's a good chance to mingle with political friends and foes on a congenial basis. Former members are invited.

The President always shows up to shake hands and "be a nice guy." The House photographer has five cameras hanging around his neck and a pocketful of film. It's his task to be sure he catches every member as he and the President smile at each other.

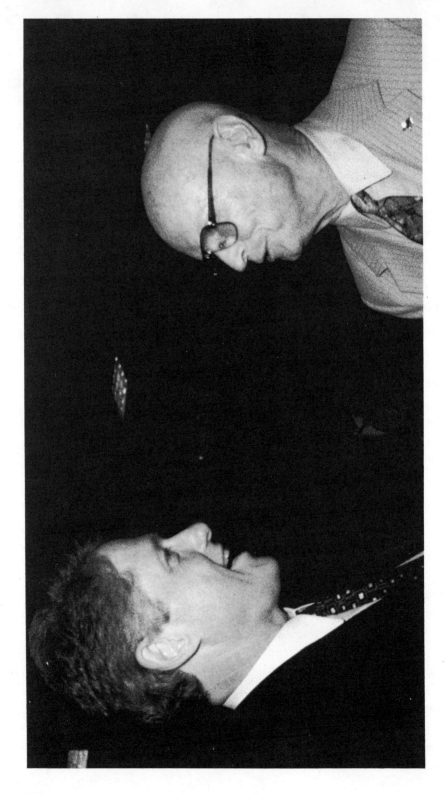

The old huckster, Bill Clinton, visits Capitol Hill, and I—despite my best intentions—find myself caught in a "Kodak moment" with him.

I have attended every one of these events for twenty-five years and have pictures with Presidents to prove it. However, in 1993, I decided I could do without a photograph of me with Bill Clinton. I had been chairman of Indiana Senior Citizens for Bush-Quayle and didn't feel a kinship with Mr. Clinton.

Because Mr. Clinton is noted for being late, I decided to attend the banquet but leave before he showed up. As I finished my dessert, I made a little speech to my dinner companions. "I'm no hypocrite," I announced. "I noticed that last year every left-wing liberal who fought against Bush rushed up to have his picture taken with him. Not me (with Clinton)! I'm out of here!"

With that I started for the door. As I was leaving, President Clinton and his entourage arrived. "Hi, I'm Bill Clinton," he greeted me, sticking out his hand.

"I'm Roger Zion," I replied with a big smile.

So, there we were...two happy people, pretending to like each other, as the cameras clicked away.

The Rayburn Room

There is a beautifully decorated room just off the house floor that is named for Sam Rayburn, the Texan who was one of the most powerful and influential Speakers in history.

It serves many purposes. When Congress meets late at night, staff people can bring mail over to be signed. During the day, staff can bring constituents over to chat with members, lobbyists can plead their cause, and administration officials can meet with congressmen who have problems.

Another function of the Rayburn Room is to have receptions for celebrities. If Miss America comes from a member's district, he will invite her to the Rayburn Room to meet the members of Congress.

I have met many queens who have represented everything from Miss Apricot to Miss Xenia Festival. Among the more famous celebrities I have met are the old, redhead huckster, Arthur Godfrey, and news commentator Chet Huntley.

I have had some great experiences and met lots of interesting people during my 25 years in Washington.

When I hear people trash the Congress, I say to myself, "These members are basically good people trying to do what their constituents demand of them." If the institution doesn't function properly, maybe part of the blame goes to the unreasonable demands of the public.

The government can't and shouldn't be the answer to all the country's problems.

If we don't do more to solve our own problems and stop expecting our elected representatives to solve them for us, we will soon find it very difficult to entice capable people to enter the profession of politics.

Then we couldn't write stories about them.

One of the many celebrities I've had the pleasure of meeting was Arthur Godfrey.